TOTALLY YOU!

TOTALLY YOU!

EVERY GIRL'S GUIDE TO LOOKING GOOD AND FEELING GREAT!

Kate Tym

Illustrated by
Gillian Martin

SCHOLASTIC INC.

New York   Toronto   London   Auckland   Sydney
Mexico City   New Delhi   Hong Kong

For Sarah 'The Dudmeister' Dudman

ISBN 0-439-18033-3

12 11 10 9 8 7 6 5 4 3 2   0 1 2 3 4 5/0

Printed in the U.S.A.   40

First Scholastic printing, February 2000

The moral rights of the author and illustrator have been asserted.
Cover photograph: Cathy Gratwicke
Cover design by Mandy Sherliker and Ness Wood
Text design by Mandy Sherliker and Ness Wood

Contents

1. Introduction

You're amazing! You're unique! You're you! Human beings come in all shapes and sizes with different personalities, opinions and rules to live by. No matter what sort of society you live in, or what you look like, one thing's for certain – there's no one else like you anywhere else in the whole wide world. And whoever you are and whatever you look like, your very individuality makes you special.

Yep, it's your body and you can really enjoy making the most of it with this head-to-toe and inside out guide to feeling fabulous and looking great. Getting in shape can be great fun and with loads of tips for DIY treats and techniques for looking after the inner you too, you can have the confidence to take care of yourself in body *and* in spirit.

So, make the most of it. Treat yourself good from the inside out and just enjoy being *Totally You!*

2. Sleep On It

Ever had a really bad night's sleep and had to struggle through the next day with a foggy head, heavy limbs and an irritation factor that's right off the scale? That's because your body's trying to tell you to get back in the sack and sort yourself out.

Sleep is top of the list of things we need to look good and feel great. Sleep gives the body a well-deserved rest after all the exertions of the day. But it's not just your body it sorts out, it's your mind too. Even though you might think you never dream, you do! Everybody does. You just might not remember your dreams, that's all. Sleeping is a fantastic way to help you sort out problems and upsets without consciously knowing you're doing it. Ever gone to bed feeling really down about something and woken up the next morning, the sun streaming through the curtains, to find that it doesn't seem nearly as bad after all?

Sleep comes in two basic forms: light and deep. You switch between the two all night. When you wake up and feel like you've had no sleep at all, but have spent the whole night tossing and turning, you probably have slept, but it's all been light sleep and it's a really decent deep sleep that you need to get you through the day.

Another thing you might have noticed, a bad night's sleep can often equal pimples or a cold sore. These can be symptoms of being run-down and being run-down usually means being tired, whacked-out and basically plain exhausted! ie – in need of a decent night's sleep or two!

If you're tired, there's nothing to be gained from staying up late. Sleep is lovely – enjoy it!

Hot Tips for a sound night's sleep

Have a bedtime routine

It makes you feel calm and secure if everything is in order just before you go to bed. So put your jammies on, brush your teeth, wash your face, open the window a touch and slide on into the sack. Your mind will take in all the cues that it's time to go the land of dreams and you'll be sleeping like a baby in no time.

Go to bed when you're tired!

If you're feeling really tired, you've had a heavy week and you're totally whacked out ... go to bed! Don't stay up to watch a late show, don't try to cram in a bit more work, don't arrange to go over to your buddy's till late... Go to bed.

Be tired when you go to bed

If you've had an active day, rushing around, playing a sport, using your brain, having fun ... you'll be more than ready for a lovely load of zzzzs. If you've been a couch potato, you'll be more likely to toss and turn with all that energy you failed to burn during the day.

Say yes to milk

If you want a bedtime snack, have something soothing and sleepy. A glass of warm milk or a cup of chamomile tea will do the trick perfectly. And avoid eating a big meal too close to bedtime, too – all that digesting'll keep you awake.

Have a cozy bed and a cool room

It's lovely to lie in a toasty bed, with warm feet and a snug bod, but if your room's too warm, you'll end up with a head full of cotton balls. Always have the window open, even if it's just a crack. A nice dose of fresh air is vital for a good night's sleep.

Cuddle up to teddy

You're never too old for a snuggly friend. Beddy-byes is a time for comfort, security and relaxation. And if Little Bear makes you feel loved then don't be afraid to give him a hug ... all night long.

Tidy up!

A messy bedroom is not a calm environment. Clambering across the junk on the floor makes you feel stressed, plus having it all looming over you, knowing you've got to clear it up and knowing that your mom's going to go nuclear about it in the morning is not good for your r and r. Fortunately, it's one problem that's easily solved. Pick those clothes up girl and get tidy!

Color me calm

Is your room in need of a touch up? Go for sleep-inducing shades. Blue is calm, yellow happy, pink is cozy and white is fresh. Steer away from depressingly dark or cold colors.

Turn off the TV

TV is a stimulant. Try not to watch anything for an hour before you go to bed. Listen to some relaxing music instead, read a book or ... some poetry! Honestly, it'll send you to sleep in no time at all!

Banish worries

If anything's preying on your mind, write it down and put the list to one side to be dealt with in the morning. This should help you stop turning it over and over in your head once you hit the sack.

> All the ingredients for a perfect night's sleep. Your body's going to thank you for it a squillion times over!

3. Work That Bod!

You might be a sport-a-holic already, in which case all there is to say is Good For You! Because it is just that: good for you. Our bodies are incredible machines, which will go on working for us throughout our lives, but we have to keep our side of the bargain. And looking after your body includes keeping it fit and healthy.

You might be the sort of person who hates all sports and would rather curl up on the couch with a pizza and video than ever darken the doorway of a gym or roller rink. The good news is that exercise comes in all shapes and sizes and if you try out enough different activities, you never know, you might just find one you like and one that you're good at too. And the brilliant thing about exercise is that it's addictive; doing exercise makes you feel good, not just physically, but mentally too. Exercise triggers the release of natural endorphins into your brain – and they're like a little injection of hormonal happy factor, so you'll be healthy, fit and smiling too!

And remember you can be fit and can feel good about yourself, knowing you're unique, you're special and you're you – and that should be more than enough for anybody!

HOT TIP

You can exercise without even knowing it – even a boogie at a party will give your heart and lungs a bit of a going over. Here are some ideas for no-effort exercise.

★ Don't get in the elevator or on the escalator ... use the stairs.

★ Don't use the bus for a five-minute journey. Turn it into a twenty-minute walk instead.

★ Don't get your mom to drive you everywhere. Get your bike out of the shed, dust down your helmet and get pedaling. It's better for the environment too!

★ If you make a regular journey that's just too far to walk or cycle, why not get off a couple of stops early and walk the final stretch? If it adds 10 minutes and you do it

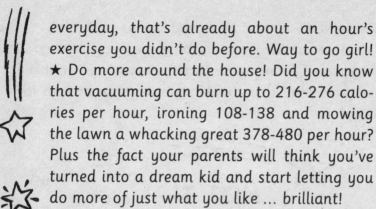

everyday, that's already about an hour's exercise you didn't do before. Way to go girl!

★ Do more around the house! Did you know that vacuuming can burn up to 216-276 calories per hour, ironing 108-138 and mowing the lawn a whacking great 378-480 per hour? Plus the fact your parents will think you've turned into a dream kid and start letting you do more of just what you like ... brilliant!

★ If you really can't handle taking the stairs instead of the escalator (shame on you by the way!) try combining both by walking up the escalator. At least you'll get a teensy bit of exercise and you'll get where you're going double quick too!

Who Told You That?

Exercise'll make me hungry, so I'll eat more. Nah, wrong again. Exercise actually makes you less hungry, but if you do a lot of it, yes, you'll be able to eat a bit more without gaining weight. Bonus!

A problem shared...

I've always liked the idea of going running but whenever I've tried it I'm out of breath and exhausted after a quick sprint around the block. Where am I going wrong?
Kay, Massachussetts

Well, first off, good for you! Secondly, don't panic! It's true running is a really effective form of exercise but, like most things, it helps if you take it easy to begin with and then build up. Don't go for an all out four-minute mile instantly. Start by picking a route that will take you about 20 minutes to half an hour. Don't run the whole way to begin with but divide your time between running and walking. So run for a couple of minutes and then walk for the next minute, then run again for two, and so on. Each time you go out, increase your running times and decrease your walking times by a little. You'll be amazed how quickly you're whizzing around the whole way. Try varying your route to keep it interesting and, if you can find a willing accomplice, go along with a friend for added motivation. By the way, make sure you're wearing a suitable pair of shoes and always let someone know exactly where you're going before you set off.

If you're planning on making a swim a regular thing why not splash out (groan!) on a swim cap and a pair of goggles. Stinging eyes and dry hair will be a thing of the past and you'll find yourself in the fast lane in no time at all!

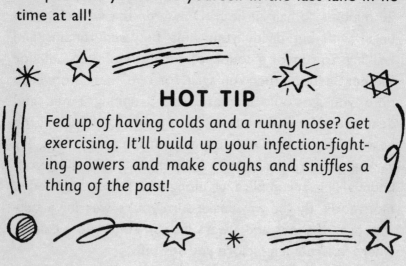

HOT TIP

Fed up of having colds and a runny nose? Get exercising. It'll build up your infection-fighting powers and make coughs and sniffles a thing of the past!

Make a day of it

Why not organize some fun days out with the gang – hey, in between shopping trips of course! Try out different stuff and see what you like best. You could each choose something you'd like to try and the others have to give it a go too. Even if it's only once a month, you'll have a whole catalog of activities to choose from. Here are some ideas:

 • Take a dance class. Whether you're interested in salsa, tap or flamenco, there's bound to be a school near you. Check out the beginners' class and see what you think. Watch out, here comes the next Darcey Bussell!

 • Go trampolining. You don't need any special clothing, it's easy to do and it's really great fun too. Lots of leisure centers now have trampolines, so find out the class times and go and give it a try. All that flying through the air will leave you all high as kites, I'll bet.

• Get your skates on. Whether it's ice, roller or in-line it's great for you and it's great fun, too. Any skating center will have skates for hire, so you don't have to fork out for your own pair until it's something you're sure you can't live without. The added bonus is that loads of gorgeous guys hang out at skating rinks too. Ooooh!

• On your bike. If you live in the city, arrange a bike ride in the countryside or find some safe cycle routes and check out your town. If you live in the country, what are you waiting for? Pack a picnic in your saddlebags and head for the open fields. There's nothing like pedaling along in the sunshine with a cool breeze in your hair to make you feel alive. Make sure that at least one of you knows how to read a map though! And always tell someone the route you intend to take.

• Hike it. OK, so hiking might have a bit of a nerdly image, but when you're up at the top of that hill admiring the view as it pans out around you, you won't feel nerdy, you'll feel fantastic. You might need a bit of help to get this one off the ground – someone with a car to get you there, someone with good map-reading skills ... If all that's a bit much to come up with, pick an easy ramble nearer to home, take your lunch and get walking. Again, always let someone else know exactly where you're off to.

• Swim it. Swimming is a great form of exercise and it's also great fun. If you don't feel like straight lane swimming, go to a leisure pool and check out the wave machines and the slides. Just climbing the stairs to get there'll do you heaps of good and again, swimming pools can score quite high on the fit boy factor.

Who Told You That?

Being thin equals being fit. Nope! If you're a skinny-minnie who never gets their butt off the couch, you ain't necessarily fit. Being thin does not necessarily equal being fit. You can be heavy and still be fit and you can be thin as a rake and as unhealthy as a pipe-smoking 80-year-old who's never done a day's work in his life! You may be slim, but if you can't run up the stairs without having to camp out in the middle to get your breath back, you certainly aren't fit — now move it!

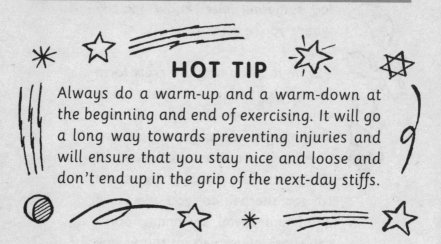

HOT TIP

Always do a warm-up and a warm-down at the beginning and end of exercising. It will go a long way towards preventing injuries and will ensure that you stay nice and loose and don't end up in the grip of the next-day stiffs.

What's Your Sport?

Not sure what's the exercise for you? Haven't got a clue whether you'd like to try your hand at tennis or check out some fancy soccer footwork? Take the test and see what's the sport for you – you'll get a bit of arm exercise while you're at it...

1. Sport's day's looming. Do you:
A. Sign up for as many events as possible – you've got the will to win?
B. Only pick the thing you know you have a flair for?
C. Pretend to tie your shoes while the volunteering's going on, so you definitely don't get picked?

2. Do you like sports because:
A. They're on TV so you don't have to get out of your chair to get involved?
B. They're competitive and give you something to strive for?
C. They're team-building and give you a sense of belonging?

3. Have you got:

A. Long arms?

B. Strong legs?

C. A small, wiry body frame?

4. When it comes to being picked for teams do you:

A. Desperately want to be picked?

B. Not mind either way. You're happy being picked but you're just as happy kicking a ball around on your own?

C. Only want to be picked for left back ... left back in the changing rooms that is!?

5. You've taken up a new sport and the time has come to invest in some equipment. Do you:

A. Save up – you take your sport seriously so you want to have the best?

B. Give it up – if it hurts your purse it ain't the sport for you?

C. Buy the cheapest stuff available. Why invest in the best when you might go off it at any moment?

6. Are you:

A. Adventurous – you like to get out and about and do things your own way?

B. Analytical – you like structures, strategies and complicated procedures?

C. Tired – even the eye-exercise you're getting reading this quiz makes you long for some zees?

7. Do you have:

A. Good balance and co-ordination?

B. Buckets of stamina – you can keep going for hours?

C. No energy and absolutely no will-power!?

8. Do you have:

A. Great hand to eye co-ordination – if anyone throws anything at you, you can catch it before you blink?

B. A great talent for procrastination – why do today what you can put off for life?

C. Great self-motivation – if you set your mind to do something, it's as good as done?

Your Sportster Scores

1. A10 B7 C3 2. A3 B10 C7 3. A9 B4 C7
4. A10 B7 C2 5. A10 B3 C7 6. A7 B10 C2
7. A10 B7 C4 8. A7 B10 C4

1-28 Competition Queen

Have a go at any team game and you're bound to be a success but one-on-one will also cater for your competitive edge. You like to judge yourself against other people and it motivates you to try harder and perform better. It's great that you're so keen to do well and it makes life very easy to choose a sport to suit you, as you'll probably succeed to a certain degree at anything you try your hand at. So try and find a couple of things you really, really like and then go for it. But don't forget, it's meant to be fun too. Don't get so hung up on coming first that you forget how to enjoy yourself along the way!

29-56 Lone Star

You're a sporty type but not that crazy to compete. Why not take up activities that you can do just for fun without having to add up a score at the end. Try cycling, or swimming, or even something like trampolining or skating. For the more adventurous among you, why not have a go at rock-climbing or scuba diving – you can usually train to do that at the local swimming pool even if you live hundreds of miles away from the nearest sea. Even if you don't really like competition there's nothing to stop you competing with yourself just to spice things up that little bit. See if you can beat your best time, or swim those few extra lengths or climb just that little bit higher. Once you get started you'll be amazed how far you can go!

57-80 Sport Avoider

Surely nobody can really be as out-and-out unmotivated as you! Make life easy on yourself why don't you and pick something that requires the least amount of investment on your time and energy. Start with walking or swimming, something that you can do on your own, you don't have to compete with anyone else and you don't need to make any investment in terms of fancy equipment or hire charges. Start small so that you're not intimidated before you start. If you've got an equally unmotivated friend, try starting out together. You can really encourage each other to keep on going. Promise yourself to walk one route a week that you would usually take the car or bus for (aim for about 20 minutes walking time if possible). Because you've set yourself a really achievable goal, you'll feel an instant success and then you can start building on it. The first time you go swimming, set yourself a low target (say five lengths) then increase it by a length each time you go – you'll be up to ten lengths in no time at all! From tiny acorns, mighty oaks do grow – so, plant those fitness acorns, you could be a top athlete just waiting to be discovered!

Top-to-Toe

If you fancy working out at home, there are always loads of exercises shown in women's magazines – again, see if your mom will let you sabotage hers so you can start an exercise file and pick and choose what you fancy doing.

Here's a set of top-to-toe exercises to get you started:

Remember always warm up first – don't start from cold!

Arms and Shoulders
Push-ups!

Yes, I know, they're hard work! But you can build up to the real toughies. Start by doing your push-ups standing up against a wall – it's much easier than the floor variety. And when you're strong enough you can always progress down to ground level!

1. Put your feet in parallel and at about hip width.
2. Stand facing the wall, far enough away that when you put your arms out in front of you and your palms flat on the wall, your arms are straight.
3. Bend your arms (without moving your feet!) so that your whole upper body moves towards the wall. Don't bend your spine but hold it straight using your tummy muscles.

4. When your nose is almost touching the wall — push back to a standing position.
5. Repeat slowly 20 times!

Waist

Any twisting from your midriff will give your waist a whittle. Here's one to be going on with:

Side bends

1. Stand with your feet apart and your hands by your side.
2. Bend to the left from the waist – reach down your left leg with your left arm. Bend your right arm at the elbow and raise it a little.
3. Gently ease the push further down your leg, finally bringing your right arm over your head – hold for around a count of ten.

4. Slowly come back to the central standing position.

5. Repeat the action on the other side.

6. Repeat both sides ten times.

NB – Be sure not to lean forwards or backwards whilst doing this. The movement is sideways only.

Tummy

When exercising your tummy it's important both your stomach muscles and back are supported so that you can't injure yourself by mistake! That's why a lot of tummy exercises take place on the floor.

The rocker

1. Lie flat on the floor, on a comfy mat or towel.
2. Bend your legs so your feet are flat on the ground and your knees are pointing at the ceiling.
3. Tuck your pelvis under so that your pelvic bone points upward and your tummy is tucked in.
4. Roll your head and shoulders off the ground, pointing your arms straight out in front of you towards your knees. Your chin should be as close to your chest as you can get it.
5. Rock in this position for a count of ten then slowly and in control, roll back down.
6. Repeat entire exercise five times.

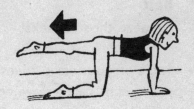

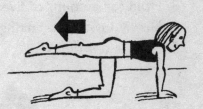

Thighs

Here's a fun and energizing exercise to give your thighs a toning treat.

1. Kneel on all fours (keep your back flat and straight). Bend your left knee, bringing it up to your chest, then push it backwards so that the leg is in a straight line with the back.
2. Hold for a count of five.
3. Without touching the floor again with your left knee, repeat ten times.
4. Do the same with the other leg.

Butt

Squeeze those cheeks!

1. Lie on your back, knees bent, arms out to the side with your palms facing downwards.
2. Raise your buttocks off the floor and raise your heels at the same time.
3. Hold for a count of five.
4. Slowly lower to starting position.
5. Repeat ten times.

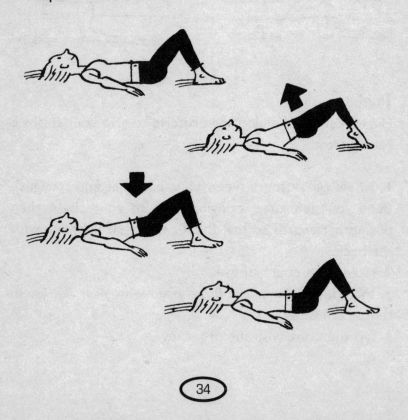

4. Feed Your Face

Food, food, food, food, food! We're bombarded with images of it daily. Buy this! Eat that! This is even more delicious than ever! Fancy packaging and ever more inventive combinations of ingredients are tempting us at every turn. But the simple fact remains that in order to eat healthily and well, you need to go back to basics.

Let's face it, when girl-kind first roamed the earth they couldn't pop into the local burger joint for a quarter-pounder and fries, donuts had definitely not been invented and the only frozen product available was a dinosaur that didn't make it through the ice-age. But good old mother nature in all her wisdom had provided for her children in other ways. The world is one big natural supermarket, perfectly designed to keep us full, fit and healthy. And it still holds true today that the more natural and less processed your food is, the better it is for you.

Before you go into panic mode at the thought of never eating a delicious piece of cake or a ready-made meal again, don't worry, it's not as heavy as all that. Every now and again it's absolutely A-OK to eat whatever you desire but, if possible, it's better to try and avoid having heavily processed or refined foods as the mainstay of what you eat.

Nobody should ever have to diet!!! Certainly not when they are still growing. Maintaining a healthy 'diet' doesn't mean going without food or even going without things you like, it simply means having a little think about what you're eating and enjoying things that are good for you too!

Foodstuffs are divided up into categories. Foods in different categories provide you with different things.

Proteins

Including: Meat, fish, poultry
Dairy products: Milk, cheese, eggs, yogurt
Grains, nuts and seeds
And in some vegetables, eg avocado pear

Proteins are the body's building blocks. They build and repair body tissue, and are a good energy provider.

Carbohydrates

There are three different types:

Sugars: Including fruits, honey and, of course, sugar!

Starches: Whole grains (wholemeal bread), cereals, pasta, rice. Root vegetables such as potatoes, carrots and parsnips. Beans, peas and pulses (lentils and that kind of thing)

Cellulose: This includes most vegetables and quite a number of fruits (which can fall into the cellulose and sugar categories). Basically, when people talk about fiber or roughage they are talking about this type of carbohydrate. They provide bulk to your diet and are necessary in keeping your digestive tract in tip-top condition

Carbohydrates really are top foods. The sugar carbohydrate foods provide energy quickly but at an acceptable level (unlike a processed sugary product which will give your body a bit of an overload). The starches are a brilliant source of energy, and it's slow-burning so you won't get a quick rush followed by a trough of exhaustion, but will be able to keep going for hours (lots of stamina-needing athletes eat an awful lot of pasta!). And the cellulose is vital for keeping everything moving ... if you see what I mean! What an excellent form of fodder!

Fats

There are two types of fat: saturated fats and unsaturated. Saturated fats are usually solid at room temperature and come from an animal source, eg lard, butter, suet. Unsaturated fats are usually liquid at room temperature and come from a vegetable source. These include olive oil (very tasty!), corn oil, sunflower oil and various nut oils and seed oils (sesame seed oil is delicious poured lightly over salad leaves)

Basically unsaturated fats are better for you than saturated fats. You don't have to never eat saturated fat again, but be aware that you should avoid eating it all the time and rather go for unsaturated fats wherever possible, but a bit of butter on your bread is not the end of the world.

Fats are not easily utilized by your body. They tend to be stored for leaner times. Women, in particular, carry their fat reserves around their tummies, butts and upper thighs. But this 'pear' shape is actually perfectly natural and healthy, it's where your fat is meant to be! Fat is not a bad thing, it protects your vital organs, and insulates your body against cold. Also, fats act as carriers for fat-soluble vitamins, which you wouldn't get from other sources. The trouble with fat is, because it's stored, if you keep eating more of it than you can use in terms of energy, it'll simply stick around until you fall on harder times. So, try not to over-do it.

Refined products:

The every-now-and-again foods, not a good foundation for a really healthy diet:

White flour / white bread	Many desserts
White sugar	Ready-made meals
Sugar-coated cereals	
Sweets / candies	
Pastries	
Cakes	
Cookies	

Eating Right is Easy

It's no hardship to eat a healthy diet, there's loads of delicious stuff out there to feed on and there's no need to feel hungry at any time if you're eating a proper well-balanced diet. In fact, you'll probably feel fuller, as the type of foods you'll be eating will be good and satisfying.

Three meals a day...

Snacking's fine, but ... most of the snacks available to buy as you make your way through the day just aren't that good for you. It's a false economy to miss breakfast and then feed your face with junk for the rest of the morning. Why not start the day as you mean to go on. How about some seasonal fruit, a yogurt, some wholemeal bread and a boiled egg?

Commercial granola/muesli tends to be packed chock full of refined sugar. Why not make your own for a healthy alternative. I bet even Dad'll be sneaking a bowlful before the week's out!

DIY Treat - Make your own granola/muesli

Mix together any of the following:
Oats
Wheatgerm
Dried apricots
Hazelnuts / almonds
Raisins / currants / sultanas
Dried banana

If there's anything else you particularly like, such as dates or different types of nuts, mix 'em on in. Note down your combinations and then when you find one you really like you'll know how to recreate it. Why not eat your granola/muesli with some fresh fruit or mix it with some yogurt for a really delicious start to the day?

So that's breakfast sorted! Don't worry if you're not keen on the cold cereal route – how about some oatmeal or a poached egg on wholemeal toast. Or, for a real savory start to the day, some grilled tomatoes on wholemeal toast. Or a combination...There must be something you like!

Lunch

Sandwiches and salads are perfect to get you through the afternoon. Remember wholemeal bread is much better than white, and lean meats, skinless chicken or flaky fish can make yummy fillings. Veggie fillings are great too, eggs provide protein and humus gives a girl a tasty lunchtime treat. Pig out on as much fruit as you like or make your own fruit salad and take it with you in a well-sealed plastic container.

Be as daring as you like with your salads and your sandwiches. Try different combos and jot down what you like best. Remember fresh herbs such as basil and parsley can give salads and sandwiches a real flavor boost.

Dinner

Why not volunteer to cook dinner one night a week? You can research your meals through recipe books from the local library and women's magazines are great places to find healthy and delicious ideas for evening meals too. Shopping for ingredients is a great way to find out about foods. Read the labels, they're very informative about sugar, salt and fat contents and will usually tell you the calorific value too. Over the weeks you'll be able to build up quite an impressive recipe file and the rest of your family will probably be begging to eat your tasty treats every night of the week.

Here's a quick 'n' easy recipe to get you going!

Creamy Mushys on Toast (Serves 4)

Served with a large salad or steamed vegetables you've got a really quick and easy and totally yummy dinner!

1 teaspoon/15g butter or margarine

1 onion thinly sliced

5 cups/350g mushrooms

2 tablespoons chopped fresh thyme

4 tablespoons chopped fresh parsley

2 cups/250g cottage cheese

4 tsp Dijon mustard

8 large slices wholemeal bread – toasted

Melt the butter/marg in a frying pan on low. Put in the onion, fry for a minute or so to soften. Turn the heat up to medium. Add the mushrooms and herbs and stir for around 5 minutes or until the mushrooms look nicely cooked. Mix in the cheese and mustard. Warm through for a minute longer. Spread the toast with butter/marg, pile the mushy mix on top and serve. Yum yum!

This is just delish with broccoli or corn on the cob! You can use the basic mix in other ways too. Add some cooked chicken and you've got a whole new meal. Try serving it on cous-cous or rice with a big salad.

Why not make an enormous fruit salad for dessert? Put in all your favorite fruits – they'll taste even better in a combi than they do on their own!

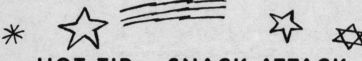

HOT TIP – SNACK ATTACK

Feel hungry between meals? Fancy a snack? That's just fine, but why not go for some healthy options; fresh fruit, dried fruit (prunes and apricots are yum-my!), cheese, raisins or nuts are good and nourishing for between-meal fillers. Bananas are so fabulous, they actually contain a substance which triggers the release of happy hormones in your brain when you eat them, so you'll end up smiling too!

You Are What You Drink

Did you know that your body is around 85 percent aqua! And, it's also one of the best things for it. Those in the know recommend that you drink about a liter and a half a day at least and even more than that if you do a lot of sports and exercise. It's brilliant stuff for washing impurities out of your body, keeping your kidneys in peak condition, keeping your skin supple, your nails strong and your hair lush and lovely. Brilliant stuff and if you get it straight from the fountain – it's even free!

Alternatively ... Drink loads of fizzy, soft drinks and go for the full sugar-rush, millions of hollow calories and the kind of tooth-decay that sends a dentist into a deep and lasting depression ... The choice is yours!

Fruit cocktails and delicious milk shakes are two great ways to take on loads of vitamins and minerals. You can experiment with different combinations and see which ones you like best – try swapping recipes with your pals.

Here are some great energy-boosting drinks we made earlier.

Banana Peanut Supreme
1 cup of milk
1 cup of yogurt (plain is fine, but if you want an extra bananary drink go for some banana yogurt)
1 banana
1 tablespoon peanut butter

Toss 'em in a blender and whizz them into submission.

Totally Tropical Treat
1 banana
1 small can pineapple chunks (in juice not in syrup)
1 mango
1 cantaloupe melon

Stick 'em in the blend and hit go.
This drink is really versatile, add in any of your favorite fruits for a different taste sensation. To make it a really special treat, you can even add in some coconut milk and drift away in a Caribbean dream!

Veg Head

If you like tomato juice or have a craving for savories, why not give this a whirl.

4 tomatoes
1 stick of celery (finely sliced)
1 carrot – grated
1 red pepper
Dash of Worcester / Tabasco sauce
(optional)

Again, if you fancy adding any other of your favorite veggies for a different flavor, give it a try. They have to have quite a high liquid content and be palatable eaten raw!

Give your own a try and remember, if you don't think it's sweet enough as is, try adding a bit of honey rather than sugar. It's unrefined so it's better for you and it has wonderful antibiotic properties – marvelous!

5. The Skin You're In

Your skin is your body's largest organ. It's responsible for keeping your temperature balanced, taking the brunt of anything thrown at you and generally keeping everything hanging together as it should. It breathes, it feels and it is constantly growing – shedding dead cells as new ones make their way to the surface.

Over your life your skin will evolve and change – look at old people's skin, it is dryer and less elastic than yours. During teenage years the skin can go through its trickiest time. Some adolescents get off pretty lightly with the odd pimple here and there and some end up in trauma-corner with grease, blackheads and acne taking over their lives. It's your hormones that will be causing all these problems. They start sending messages to your body to sort your skin out ready for adult life – giving men a coarser-looking skin than women – but between the ages of about 12 to 16, it doesn't always get it right and while your body's searching for the right balance, your skin looks like a war-zone for the battling hormones. But, don't throw the towel in yet. You don't need to lock yourself in a dark room for four years, it's definitely not as bad as all that. It may not be the greatest time for you skin-wise, but there's still a lot you can do to control problems and sometimes prevent them before they even begin.

What Type are You?

Skins come in different colors and textures and knowing your type means that you can take the best care of it.

Skin Type
Oily
- Do you get a shiny nose and forehead?
- Is dry flaky skin something you know nothing about?
- Are you prone to blackheads and pimples?

Dry
- Does your skin feel tight after washing, even with the mildest of facial washes?
- Do you get itchy flaky patches?

Combination
- Do you get a greasy forehead and nose but find your

cheeks feel dry and tight?

Balanced

- Is your skin perfect - never dry and never oily? Well, lucky you!

Color

Light

- You may have very fair, very dark or red hair. You burn easily in the sun and don't tend to get a very deep tan. You may be prone to having slightly drier skin.

Medium

- You can burn but will tan fairly easily.

Dark

- You very rarely burn, you tan easily, you may be prone to having slightly oilier skin. You will tend to have dark hair and eyes.

Black

- The term 'black' covers many more shades of skin than the term 'white' from dark olivey skin-tones through to velvety ebonies. You don't burn easily but can be subject to skin damage from prolonged sun exposure.

Skin Care

When you are young, your skin is still settling down and you may not know your true 'type' until you are in your early twenties when your hormones finally settle down into the order you will more-or-less have for life. Because of this, it is often true to say that when caring for your skin the less you do is often the better. If you over-wash, or cleanse or use harsh toners or astringents because you feel your skin is greasy, this can lead to your skin over-compensating and producing more and more oil ... blocking more and more pores and giving you more and more pimples! It is true that the best way to prevent pimples is to keep your skin clean and grease-free but you don't need to go overboard. A gentle facial wash is the best thing to use – first thing in the morning and last thing at night. Only wash your face more regularly if you've been exercising or doing something a bit messy... euwww!

Cleanse, Tone and Moisturize

It's a good idea to have a basic skin-care routine that you can stick to. If you try lots of different lotions and potions lots of times a day, your skin won't know if it's coming or going. Try out a few different products (get recommendations from friends) and then once you've found something you and your skin seem to get along with – stick with it. Unless you do a lot of sports, it's fine to wash your face twice a day (when you get up and before you go to bed) and, on days when you're going out for a special evening, give your face another wash just before you go out.

Cleanse...

A pH balanced or gentle face wash will do. And remember: rinse, rinse, rinse – any residue left on your skin can lead to blocked pores and pimples. Pat your face dry with a lovely soft towel – don't rub it – your facial skin is very delicate and won't appreciate rough treatment.

If you've worn make-up, you might want to use a make-up remover first to get off the majority of your make-up before washing your face.

Tone...

If you have oily skin or suffer from spots or pimples, it can be a good idea to wipe your skin over with a mild toner. Don't go for anything too astringent as you don't actually want to disrupt the skin's balance too much or disturb the 'acid mantle' of the skin – the natural protective covering that helps fight bacteria. A quick whisk over with some witch hazel on a cotton ball will be more than enough.

If you don't suffer from pimples or your skin is dry you may not feel the need to tone at all. Although it does make sure the skin is completely cleansed it is not essential, so if you feel happier not toning, don't do it!

Moisturize...
This is great for everyone. Moisturizers, despite their name, don't actually introduce moisture into the skin. They are there more as a protective layer, trapping in the skin's natural moisture and protecting against the buffeting your skin gets throughout the day from the sun, wind and rain.

You can apply your moisturizer after cleansing and toning (if you do it) to your lovely clean skin. Just dab a little on your chin, forehead, nose and cheeks and rub it in gently until it disappears. You won't need to use a lot and a good moisturizer should feel as if it's been completely absorbed – as if you're not wearing any at all.

You can get different moisturizers for different skin types so be sure to choose the type that is suitable for you.

Exfoliate....
Every couple of weeks it's a good idea to have a bit of an

exfoliating scrub to get rid of dead cells that might be hanging around waiting to block up all those pores. If you don't feel like investing in an expensive skin treatment, just go for run of the mill kitchen salt. Loads of expensive beauty salons will actually sell you this as a treatment!

Give your face a wash as normal, then soak your face cloth in warm water, sprinkle salt on it and gently rub this over your whole face. You need only rub gently for a short time and then give your face a thorough rinse with clean water. Your skin should feel smooth and tingly. It'll be totally debris free and ready to face everything the world has to throw at it for the next couple of weeks.

DIY Treat

Ground-up chick peas make a great exfoliating scrub. Drain 'em from the can, mash 'em up, rub and rinse - lovely!

Pimple Alert!

Everybody gets pimples at some time or another. But in your teenage years they can come on extra strong as your body tries to make a break for adulthood, releasing a flood of hormones into your system which give confusing messages to oil-producing glands in your skin (sebaceous glands) to go into mass production. Often, too much oil is then produced and your pores can get blocked and infected and ... you've pimples to be proud of.

Pimples are not about being dirty or about being piggy when it comes to chocolates or greasy snacks. They can be influenced by external factors, but they're not caused by them. So, a healthy diet, regular exercise and a sensible cleansing routine can help you control your pimples and will help with your overall health and appearance.

Keeping on top of pimples

• Eat well and play well. If you're in the peak of health, you'll be able to get a better idea of just how bad your pimple problem is. Run-down skin is more prone to blemishes and so keeping fit and eating well will give you a clearer idea of what's up with your skin and just how to treat it.

• Wash, but not too much. Too much cleansing can actually lead to more bodily confusion and the pro-duction of more and more oil. Keep to a normal twice-a-day cleansing routine and avoid soap and soap-based products, as they can be too harsh for your skin. Try using a gentle face wash or one that is pH balanced.

• Exfoliate. Spotty skin sheds cells at a slower rate than more balanced skin. This is a bit of a vicious circle as the fact that the dead cells don't slew off can lead to blocked pores which can lead to ... you guessed it ... pimples! Try exfoliating once a week with a gentle exfoliating lotion or a facial brush or even plain old salt (see p60).

• Hands off. Leave your face alone. The more you touch your face the more dirt and germs you transfer to your skin and that's just what spots love to get going.   And, above all, don't squeeze them. You'll only make them worse, they'll go on for longer and you could even cause scarring. If you really, really can't resist the temptation, wait until the spot is good and ready to pop, make sure your hands are clean and then only squeeze gently – never force it and never, ever use your finger nails. Once popped pat the area with alcohol, or tea tree oil.

• Cover up. In the sun take care of your skin. Use a good quality, oil-free sunscreen. The sun can be very good for pimpley skin, but only in moderation, so take the usual precautions (see p 65). Remember if you are taking any medication for your skin, it can often make it more sensitive, so be extra careful.

• Hide and disguise. If you really can't face the world when you've got a big whopper right in the middle of your forehead, remember there are loads of great concealing make-ups out there just to help you through the day.

• Seek help. If you're really suffering and find that the odd pimple has turned into something rather more serious and rather more permanent, don't be afraid to seek advice. Your doctor can help and there are plenty of skin specialists out there who can't wait to get their hands on your face, back and chest. Your skin might not clear up instantly, but within about two months you should see a marked improvement. It's worth the embarrassment isn't it?

A problem shared...

I've got pretty OK skin on the whole - a bit oily but nothing I can't handle. But the blackheads on my nose are U-G-L-Y! I've tried squeezing them, but my nose just ends up looking all red and blotchy and then it goes all dry and peely. What can I do to clear my blackheads up without ending up looking like Rudolph?
Sasha, Mechanicsville

Please don't squeeze! Blackheads are oil plugs in the pores that blacken on exposure to air. The black has nothing to do with dirt; it's the result of oxidization. Too much pressure can rupture the pore wall and spread bacteria underneath the skin's surface, which could cause a major breakout. Also, it can cause broken capillaries and even leave fine scarring so, best avoided at all costs! The good news is that you don't need to employ bullyboy tactics to get rid of the old 'heads. Try a facial sauna followed by a cleansing mask (see p 61) every now and again, to really lift out that ingrained dirt. When time's short, though, here's another idea. There are now a few products on the market designed just to deal with blackheads and blocked pores. They come in the form of strips, which you smooth down over the affected area (nose or forehead), leave for 10-15 minutes, and then peel off, taking all the gunk with them. Why not give 'em a whirl?!

A problem shared...

Help! Overall my skin's fine, but I've got these bumpy areas on the back of my arms and on the outside of my thighs – my friends say they're not that noticeable, but I hate them - in the summer I don't even want to wear sleeveless tops! What can I do to get rid of this bumpy skin?

Mandy, Preston

Don't worry, Mandy. This one's easy-peasy. These bits of your bod are prone to poor circulation. Ever noticed on a cold day that your butt and upper thighs can take a long time to lose the chill factor? Because of this, the skin in these areas might not be as toned as elsewhere. So, invest in a loofah or a wash mitt. String or mesh soap sacks will have the same effect too. Basically any wash cloth with a slightly abrasive surface will do the trick. The action of rubbing the surface of the skin with a shower gel and a rough surface will stimulate the circulation whilst slewing off dead cells and leaving your skin silky smooth. It might not happen overnight, but soon your arms and thighs will be as good as new. And you don't have to rub too hard, just a bit of gentle pressure will be fine. Don't forget to rub on some lovely scented moisturizer afterwards – you smoothy!

DIY Treat

For your bod as well as your face, one of the best things in the world for skin is good old sodium chloride — that's salt to you and me! Yep, treating your skin to a rub-down with salt can leave it feeling smooth, silky and totally refreshed. Forget expensive treatments, just head straight for the kitchen and grab yourself a tub of salt, rub-down, rinse and hey-presto, one baby-soft body awaits.

 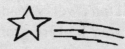

HOT TIP

Four hot tips for darker skins:

★ Darker skin is naturally shinier than paler skin. Use a mud/clay mask every couple of weeks to soak up excess oils.

★ A dusting of your favorite loose powder should combat any shine.

★ You'll look great in nearly any shade of eye shadow. But especially in pale shimmery shades as they'll contrast beautifully with your skin.

★ Darker skin marks quite easily - so leave those pimples alone!

DIY Treats

Oat, Apple and Honey Face Mask

Problem skin need not be a problem for long. There are lots of natural ingredients that have antiseptic qualities – just perfect for sorting out pimples and zapping zits. Try it and see.

Gather together:
1 apple, peeled and grated
1 teaspoon honey
Half a teaspoon single cream *
1 teaspoon ground oats
Half a teaspoon ground cinnamon

Mash the ingredients into a smooth paste using a fork. Smear it on your face – avoiding your eyes – and leave on for ten minutes. Rinse off gently with cool water, then pat dry with a clean towel. Now doesn't that feel nice!

* you can freeze the cream you don't use. If you think you'll do this recipe again, why not freeze the cream in an ice tray and then you'll have handy-sized blocks for defrosting!

As a refreshing exfoliating alternative to the above swap the cream with a tablespoon of plain live yogurt and cinnamon with 2 teaspoons of fresh lemon juice and take the honey out altogether!

Rose and Almond Hand Cream

Gather together:
$1\frac{1}{2}$ teaspoons cocoa butter
1 teaspoon beeswax (granules or grated)
2 tablespoons almond oil
3 tablespoons rosewater
Half a teaspoon baking powder
10 drops rose absolute

Melt the cocoa butter, beeswax and almond oil over a bowl of hot water. In a different bowl, heat the rosewater slightly and dissolve the baking powder into it, then stir into the cocoa butter mixture very slowly and keep stirring until the cream cools. Then add the rose absolute, stir and tip into a jar. Clean the bowls thoroughly before they cool or the mix will harden. Store your hand cream in the fridge.

DIY Treat

A couple of egg yolks with a teaspoon of honey make a great mask for dry skin. Leave on for five minutes then rinse off. Or, for oily skin, use egg whites with a teaspoon of lemon juice instead.

HOT TIP

 Get your circulation going and give your skin a healthy glow, by blasting yourself quickly with cold water at the end of your shower.

Bathing Beauty

Make the most of bath time with some yummy bubble bath. Put a capful of bubble bath into the tub as you're filling it up. To make it extra-bubbly, top up with some cold water. Warm/hot baths are better than hot-hot baths. Really hot baths dry out your skin and make your face sweaty! Stay in the bath long enough to relax but not so long that you turn into a prune. After a warm bath, your skin is really ready for all those lotions and potions you can slather on. What a smoothie!

Who Told You That?

Shaving your legs will make the hair grow back thicker. Summer's coming and you're feeling a bit fluffy? But someone told you that shaving your legs will make the hair grow back thicker. Don't you worry, shaving your legs does not change the texture of the hair. OK, when the hair starts to grow back and you're in stubble-city, it may feel thicker, but it's not. Fine hair will stay fine, and thick hair will stay thick and that goes for hair anywhere else, too! It only feels thicker because you've hacked it off right in the middle of the hair, where it is a bit thicker, and it's short, so it's sticking rigidly up. Never fear, when you give up for winter, it'll return to its pre-shave texture.

HOT TIP

For deep cleansing try a facial sauna. Get a large bowl. Pour in some very hot (but not boiling) water. Hover your face over the water with a towel tented over you and the bowl. Make sure your nose doesn't dip in the water – it's hot! Stay there for 5-10 minutes, or until there's no steam. Rinse your face with luke-warm water and moisturize as usual.

Sun-Safe

The sun's out, the sky's blue and you and your pals can't wait to hit the beach... And that's just fine, but remember to take a few things with you to make your day happy and healthy and ensure you don't get fried – nobody likes the lobster look!

It's a sad fact that too much sun just isn't good for you. We're talking premature wrinkles, hide like a rhino's and, in the worst-case scenario, even skin cancer. However, that doesn't mean you have to spend every sunny day for the rest of your life, locked in a cupboard with a full-body plastic suit on. No, you can still hit the beach, you've just got to follow a few simple rules to keep you sun-safe and smiling whatever the temperature!

• **Protect yourself.** At the start of the summer invest in a good sunscreen, at least SPF15 for ordinary use (go up to 30 if you're planning a real beach day or have fair skin).

• Apply liberally. Make sure you've spread it on all over — if you've missed a bit it'll burn. And apply it frequently — particularly if you keep going in for a dip. Remember if you're prone to break-outs, there are plenty of oil-free lotions around too, so go for one of them.

• Don't rush it. The idea is to get a bit of color in your cheeks, not roast yourself on the spit of tanning mania. Start slowly with only a bit of exposure every day. Never sit out during the hottest midday/early afternoon hours. If you're out and about at those times, cover up — a nice crisp long-sleeved white shirt and a floppy hat will do the trick.

• Don't go too low. It's recommended that you don't go below SPF 8. You'll still catch the rays through it and you'll be able to stay out longer, safely. And remember, a tan that took time to build stays longer than a rush job.

• If you do accidentally fry yourself — we've all been there. Make sure you get a soothing after-sun lotion on asap. Aloe Vera is a great natural healer for seared skin. And learn your lesson and don't do it again!

• Fake it. Hey, why be a beach slave when ten minutes in the bathroom can achieve the same. Get together with your friends, buy a different self-tanning product each, try 'em out and see who gets the best results.

HOT TIP

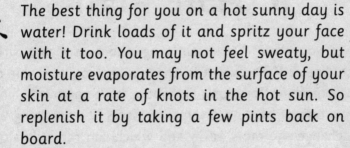

The best thing for you on a hot sunny day is water! Drink loads of it and spritz your face with it too. You may not feel sweaty, but moisture evaporates from the surface of your skin at a rate of knots in the hot sun. So replenish it by taking a few pints back on board.

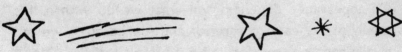

6. Hair Flair

How's your hair? Dark, fair, long, short, straight, curly, thick, fine...? Whatever it is, chances are you'll be able to find something you don't like about it! It's a weird thing, hair is one of our most versatile assets; it's the thing we can change the most easily and which can radically alter our appearance depending on what we do with it. It's usually pretty easy to care for and (unlike boys) we can usually hang on to it for life! But are we satisfied? No. If you've got curly hair you're probably jealous of your buddy whose hair's so straight it looks like she irons it. If you're a fiery redhead, you've probably always harbored a secret desire to be a bubbly blond. It seems no matter what hair we've got we always dream of having someone else's. But hey, hair's great, there's so much you can do with it. Even if you don't want to go for a radical new style, you can always wear your style in a different way: wear it up, wear it down, change where you part it.

Have fun with your hair. Change it every now and again and see how it makes you feel about the new you.

Hair Care

The best thing you can do for your hair is keep it happy and healthy and looking great. And that's not as hard as it sounds! A basic hair-care routine should keep your hair in mint condition.

• Try not to wash your hair too often. Every other day is usually fine, although if you do have rather greasy hair you might prefer to wash it every day – so pick a gentle shampoo for that.

• Pick the product that suits your hair type and don't over-use it. Remember less is more!

• Be kind when you dry. Let your hair dry naturally if you can. If it needs styling with a hairdryer, wait until it's already nearly dry before getting going.

• Get your hair cut every six to eight weeks if possible. The best thing for keeping your hair in prize-winning condition is a decent cut.

DIY Treat

Fruity Hair and Body Treatment

Treat your hair and bod to a deeply conditioning and moisturizing treat and all you need are an avocado pear and a lovely ripe mango.

Mash the avocado and mango together in a bowl – use a fork for this. Work the mixture until it's fairly nice and smooth. Then knead it into your hair and leave it for at least 15 minutes, but no longer than two hours. Then head to the bathroom and rinse it all out. Mmmmm doesn't your hair smell lovely and fruity.

Use any leftovers to give your skin a treat. Avocado's a really effective moisturizer. Leave it for half an hour or so and then ... wash it off. Don't you feel special!

QUICK FIX TIP

Going out? Hair a bit greasy? No time to wash it? Haven't got any dry shampoo? Well, reach for the talcum powder. Only use a little bit. Sprinkle it in, leave it for a minute and pat it out. Only resort to this method if you're blond though, as it can make dark-haired people look a little on the dandruffy side and that's not good!

What's the Prob?
Top tips for hassle-free hair

Dull or lifeless hair

Fed up of looking in the mirror and seeing a limp lettuce hanging on your head? Never fear ... help is here:

Dull or lifeless locks are often the result of not having chosen the right products for your hair type or just using too many – particularly things you use after the wash like mousse, gel and wax.

Sort it out!

• Get rinsing! When you wash and condition your hair it's vitally important that you get all the products out of your hair before you start drying it. Left over soapy stuff is going to leave your hair looking dull and dreary. If you find a product is almost impossible to rinse out – it's not for you – move on to something that's right for your hair.

• Rinse clean. Don't dunk your head in your dirty tub water and think that'll do it. That's fine to begin with, but keep on rinsing with some new clean water. If you're brave enough and want super sleek hair try using cold water for the final rinse. No need to go overboard though – you don't want to die of shock in the quest for better-looking hair!

• Try adding a capful of vinegar (white vinegar if you've got fair hair) to your final rinse – then you'll really shine.

• Cut down on styling products. In an attempt to give your hair more lift and life you could be doing just the opposite. The more mousse and hairspray you use on your hair, the more you'll weigh it down and leave it lank and unable to breathe. Remember the basic beauty rule ... less is always more!

• Check the label. If you know your hair, you'll know which product is right for you. If you've got dry hair, buy a shampoo that's designed for you. If you buy a shampoo for greasy hair, and your hair is dry, not only will it not improve your hair condition, but it could actually make it worse.

• Eat right. A healthy diet is good for everyone but for those of you with a dull hair problem try munching on yogurt, eggs, cereal and vegetables for an inside-out approach to hair that glows.

• If you like swimming – wear a cap! Granted, they look hideous, but it's only temporary – your hair's forever and a build-up of chlorine can really make it dull and dry.

• When you dry your hair don't towel-dry it too roughly or brush it when it's wet. Squeeze it gently through your towel and leave it to dry naturally for as long as possible before resorting to the blow dryer. Then, always angle your dryer so that the nozzle points down the hair, blowing in the direction of growth and leading to a much smoother finish.

QUICK FIX TIP

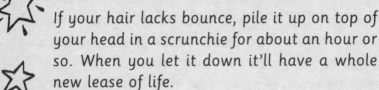

If your hair lacks bounce, pile it up on top of your head in a scrunchie for about an hour or so. When you let it down it'll have a whole new lease of life.

DIY Treat

Eggs are brilliant for giving your hair a bit of a boost. Mix two eggs with a cup of olive oil and comb the mixture through your hair. Wait 20 minutes and then wash it out and condition your hair as usual — shiny or what?!

Flyaway hair

If your hair is really fine and flyaway you may feel it's a drag. After all, every time you pull your sweater over your head you go into static overload and look like you've just stuck your finger in the electric socket! But never fear ... help is here:

Sort it out!

• Don't over-wash. This can make it fluffy and difficult to style. Only wash it every day if you really have to.

• You may dream of long locks but often for very fine hair, short is better. It gives the illusion of thickness, whereas when it's long it can look a little on the stringy side.

• If your hair is very dry, it can be prone to being a bit flighty. Use a rich but light conditioner every time you shampoo. Check out the label to find the one that's just right for you.

• Get your hair trimmed on a regular basis. Split-ends will only add to the fluffiness so get them chopped before they become a big deal. Hairdressers recommend you visit them every six to eight weeks for a tidying trim.

DIY treat

If your hair's a bit on the dry side, natural yogurt makes a great conditioner. Pick a plain one of course, you don't want lumps of strawberry stuck in your hair for weeks. Simply dump the yogurt on your hair, leave it for an hour and then rinse it out. Then shampoo and condition as normal.

Queen of Frizz

Is your hair a frizzy nightmare, fluffing out when it's dry and impossible to get your fingers through when it's wet? Well, worry not, help is at hand:

Sort it out!

- It could be that your hair is dry, dry, dry. Try using a leave-in conditioner after you shampoo.
- Heat sucks moisture out of your hair so try to use hot styling gadgets as little as possible. Leave your hair to dry naturally if you can. If it needs some styling let it get nearly dry before resorting to the hairdryer and never, ever blow-dry from wet – that spells disaster for frizz-heads.

- Try using an anti-frizz serum. But remember, a little drop is more than enough – more than that and you could end up looking like a bit of an oil slick! Serum can be particularly effective on curly or permed hair.

• Use a diffuser attachment if you have one. It's less heat intensive and kinder on your locks.

• Avoid brushing – you can end up looking like a fright-night cat's tail.

• Snip those split-ends. Head to the hairdressers every six to eight weeks and give your split-ends the chop before they completely take over and ruin your life!

DIY Treat

Lavender and Rosemary Hair Gloss

Great for calming static frizz and keeping your locks looking sleek and luscious.

Gather together:
2 tablespoons rosemary oil
1 teaspoon lavender oil

Mix the oils and store them in a small tinted bottle to protect them from light. When you've styled your hair, rub a few drops into the palm of your hands. Run your hairbrush over your palm, then brush through your hair. Lovely!

Uh-oh: Dandruff Attack!

Dandruff is the single most common scalp complaint. Don't worry though, it's not a dreadful disease or anything horribly contagious that you can catch off somebody else and it's not a sign of being dirty or not washing your hair either – even the most scrupulously clean people can suffer from a spot of the dreaded 'D'! Dandruff is simply a build-up of dead skin cells that despite normal brushing and washing, refuse to go away. No one seems quite sure why some people suffer and others don't, but it does seem that more often than not, a tendency towards greasy hair and having dandruff do seem to go together ... bummer or what!

Sort it out!

Don't panic ... it's not as bad as it seems.

You could start by trying your own home-made treatment. Use a mild shampoo and follow it up with an antiseptic treatment. So wash and condition your hair as normal and then make sure you've rinsed it really thoroughly – there's nothing more guaranteed to make your scalp itch than a build-up of residual hair-care products. Then, once you're satisfied you've got all the conditioner out of your hair, divide your hair up from the back to the front in one-inch sections.

Now, make up your lotion. Get an ordinary teacup and fill it half full with distilled water (it is important that it is distilled water and you can get this from any good chemist) then add half a cup of any good mouthwash (eg Listerine). Dip a cotton ball into your lotion and dab down the lines you've made in your hair so that your whole scalp is covered. Leave the lotion on for about half an hour – it might feel a bit tingly, which is good; if it feels uncomfortable rinse it off immediately – once the time is up give your hair a thorough rinse with clean water.

Try this a couple of times a week, and see how it goes. If you have no success, step up to phase two! There are plenty of really good medicated shampoos available that should solve the problem in no time at all. Plus the manufacturers are usually very conscious that not only do you want a healthy scalp, but you also want lovely hair, so the shampoos are designed to leave your hair looking fabulous too. Follow the instructions on the label carefully and you should be dandruff free in next to no time.

If, after trying both of the above, your dandruff shows absolutely no sign of abating, it's time to seek professional help – the dandruff might be an indication of a more serious condition. Pop along to see your family doctor who'll be able to recommend whether or not you should see a trichologist or dermatologist (both specialists in skin conditions). But, usually, it's nothing more sinister than good old dandruff and a quick course of an appropriate shampoo will have it sorted in no time.

Growing Pains

OK, so you've been trying to grow your short crop out for what seems like a century and you've been in that awkward in-between stage for life. It's not just you, I'm afraid, hair just doesn't grow as quickly as people seem to think it should! It only grows about a centimeter/half an inch a month at the best of times, so if you want it down to your waist, you're in for a long wait!

Here are a few nuggets to help you through the wait:

• There are loads of lush bits and bobs around for putting your hair up. Clip it, band it or keep it back with a zigzag strip. When your hair looks horrible down, it's the best time to have fun making it look fabulous up!

• Trim it. I know it's hard to lose an inch when it seems like it took forever to grow it, but you'll be amazed with the results. By trimming it you'll make it look thicker by getting rid of all those wispy ends, and by making it look thicker, you'll very likely make it look longer too! And if you don't get it cut, you'll end up with really long hair that's in the worst condition in the world!

• Eat well: protein helps hair grow and lots of water and fresh fruit and veg will keep it healthy too. What a great excuse for improving your diet, 'No chips for me thanks – I'm growing my hair!'

Gadget Corner

If you'd like to try curling, crimping, straightening or de-frizzing there's usually a tool for the job. But which does what and are they really necessary? Here's a de-mystifying list for the hair-care phobic!

Crimpers

If you love the zigzag effect you see on some people's heads, crimpers are the things for you. Two hot metal plates with zigzag surfaces come together with your hair sandwiched in between. Held in place for about a minute and then released, you have an instant crinkle-cut effect.

You can do loads of different things with crimpers to achieve different looks. Only do the front section of your hair instead of your whole head. If you've got medium to long hair pull it up into a high ponytail and only crimp that bit. Crimp different sections to give your head a checkerboard effect. And the great thing is, as with most gadget-produced hairstyles – as soon as you've had enough of it, it'll wash right out.

Alternatively, if you can't bear to part with the cash for a temporary thrill, get a friend to put as many little plaits or braids into your hair as she can – they should be as thin as possible for maximum effect. Do this when your hair is damp – if it's dry mist it with a plant spray. Then dry your hair thoroughly: a head canopy dryer is best for this, but if you haven't got one a hand-held dryer will do. Then take the little plaits/braids out and hey-presto! Instant crimping with no cash crisis!

Curling Iron/Tongs

A hot metal rod that you can wrap a small section of (dry) hair round to produce a curl or ringlet effect. If your hair is very straight you'll probably need a spray or mousse to help the curl stay put. Some curling irons/tongs come with different width attachments so that you can have different sizes of curls. As you have to hold the iron/tongs in place for about a minute for each curl, it can be quite a time-consuming business!

Heated Curlers

You use these on dry hair. They stay in your hair until they've cooled down, so the whole process takes quite a long time. Heated curlers will provide a gentle, bouncing curl and again, will need help from a setting spray or mousse if you really want the curl to last.

Straightening Irons

These work like crimpers only instead of having zigzag plates they have flat plates. These work brilliantly if you have slightly wavy hair and covet a sleek, shiny look as they leave your hair smooth and silky and ... straight. You can even use them to straighten out curly hair – all you need is a little patience and a lot of time!

A problem shared...

I'm always seeing models with fabulous hair piled up on their heads in magazines, but whenever I try to do it, it's a complete flop. I just can't put my hair up at all. What am I doing wrong?
Clare, Washington DC

You're probably not doing anything wrong, you have to remember that models in magazines have had someone doing their hair for them, it's probably taken hours and the stylist will come and fix it every five minutes during the photo-shoot, so that not so much as one loose hair ends up on film! But, as I assume you won't be investing in your own personal stylist, there are some things you can do to help you get your hair up and keep it staying up the whole night through!

It's actually harder to put up sleek, clean hair than hair that hasn't been washed since the day before. Clean hair is just too sleek and slides out of any style you try to inflict on it. So why not leave putting your hair up until the day after you washed it.

If your style involves starting with a high ponytail, put your hair up into it in two sections first. With long hair, it's quite heavy and one band has trouble keeping it all up. So pull the front half of your hair up into one band and the back half up into another band, beside it. And then wrap a third band around the whole tail and you'll find it's held in place much more securely.

Doing things around the back of your head is always tricky. You can't see what you're doing and have to work it all out by touch and if you do use a couple of mirrors to see, it's all back to front. So, enlist some help. See if your mom, sister or best buddy will help you out. It'll be a lot less hassle for you and they might even enjoy playing stylist for a while.

Don't forget, stylists use loads of pins, clips and spray to keep their styles in place. They may look all shiny and natural but they're probably pretty stiff to the touch. So, if you really want a style that stays, you might have to give it some spray.

Coloring

OK, so your mother might flip if you go for a full-blown new-you in the hair color stakes. But there are ways to liven up your locks without giving your parents heart failure. Know your way around the different products available and ... come up with a few ideas of your own.

Temporary / Wash-in, Wash-out Products
These are easy to use and won't (hopefully) lead you straight to the principal's office. You can usually buy them pretty cheaply in packets and they are available for blonds and brunettes. They just add a hint of a tint to your hair, without actually altering your natural color. They don't actually penetrate your locks but coat your hair, like a conditioner, so you can try one for the weekend and wash it out and be back to normal in time for class on Monday morning!

Blonds usually get to choose between strawberry tones, platinum (sort of metallicy silver) and honey tones. Whereas brunettes can go from fiery coppers to deep plummy reds. And the brilliant thing is, they're really easy to use. You just treat them pretty much like a shampoo – wetting your hair and lathering the stuff in – the only difference is you then have to sit there and let it work its magic. Leave it on for between ten and 20 minutes depending on how much color you want and then rinse. Wow! It's the new you! And in three washes it's back out and no damage done.

They're the perfect way to experiment with color without having to make a scarily life-changing decision. See if you like yourself as a raven-haired beauty before going for it full-time.

Other color fun can be had with spray colors and gels that wash out the moment you've had enough.

Semi-permanents

The next step up from wash-in wash-outs, are semi-permanent hair colors, which last for between six and twenty-four washes — best for the summer vacation perhaps. They're also a bit more tricky to use as they require mixing and can make a real mess of your bathroom towels!

You also have to check them for skin sensitivity before you even start — so always buy the kit a couple of days before you intend to use it as you'll have to do a patch test on the inside of your elbow which you leave for 48 hours to make sure you're not going to break out in a hideous rash the moment the stuff touches your head! They usually come in a box kit with full instructions on mixing the lotions and potions. You then put it on your hair like a shampoo, leave for the time instructed and rinse and rinse until the water runs clear.

Then ... let your hair dry and keep your fingers crossed you like the result!

Permanent Hair Colors

Gulp! Let's hope you've got really cool parents if you're going for this one. It really is only for those who want to change their hair forever and is, apart from anything else, an expensive path to start down on. It changes the color of the hair treated permanently. So, as soon as the new growth comes through, you can see the rather unattractive roots, so ... time to buy more product to sort your roots out, but oh, look, four weeks later more roots ... time to buy some more ... you get the picture! You're hooked – a hair color casualty. And the other thing to remember is that it's often best to get permanent coloring done by a hair-care professional, because it is permanent and so you want to make sure it's been done properly and that really is expensive!

So, if you ever do reach this stage, make sure you pick a color you know you like as there's no going back and, as you're going to all that trouble anyway, make sure you invest in a decent salon-designed shampoo to protect that color once it's in.

HOT TIP

If you are having a go at dyeing your hair at home, rub some Vaseline around your forehead and ears and it'll stop them getting tinted too! It's a good idea to put a line of cotton balls along your forehead too, to soak up any accidental dribbles and stop them getting in your eyes.

Herbal Hair Dye

The most fun thing to do — as usual — is have the satisfaction of making your own stuff. Why not have a go at enhancing your natural color with a herbal hair dye. It's easy-peasy and you can get most of the ingredients from a good health food shop.

Here are some ideas to get you started:

1 handful rosemary (smells lush!)
1 handful red clover

1 handful nettle herb
(You can always cut open nettle tea bags!)
For light hair - one handful chamomile
(it's tea-bag time again!)
For dark hair - one handful sage
For oily hair - one handful witch hazel
For dry hair - one handful marigold

Mix ingredients, then put a handful in a saucepan, add 2 cups/500ml water and bring slowly to the boil. Bubble for 15 minutes, then strain the liquid into a pitcher/jug. After shampooing and conditioning, dilute the mixture with cold water and give your hair a final rinse, catching the liquid and re-rinsing with it until you're done.

Hair Mascaras

Available in all sorts of fantastic colors – try to persuade your friends to buy some so that you can mix and match. One of the most effective looks with these is to section off two wide strips at the front of your hair and only color that. Or, if you have a fringe/bangs you can color that and two thin strands beside it for a really striking look.

Hair Color Mousses

These now come in a range of colors and some have a brush applicator so they're easy to put on.

Hair Color Sprays

Yep, you can even spray a bit of color onto your hair. Or, go for the glittery look and have a squirt of instant glamor that'll wash out just as quick!

HOT TIP

For instant root-lift turn your head upside down and blow-dry your hair with the air current blowing up against the grain of the hair. For long locks flick your head the right way up again and blow the rest of the length smoothly in the right direction for a perfect finish.

Sun Stressed Tresses

Yup, 'fraid so, wouldn't you know it, the sun's bad for your hair too! So take care of it. Too much sun beating down on your melon can leave you with dry, straw-like locks, a burnt scalp and sun-stroke – yikes! But vacations needn't be hell for hair, if you take the following advice:

- Sort your hair out before you go. If your hair's in good condition to start with it'll handle the beating it gets from the sun better than hair that's already in a state. So, go for a trim and treat it nice before you start sunning it. Try using an intensive conditioner once a week for a few weeks before your spell in the sun approaches.
- Use a leave-in conditioner – it'll provide your hair with protection round the clock.
- Wear a hat. There's nothing better for your hair than keeping out of those damaging rays altogether. So slip a hip hat on and stay super cool.
- Use a soothing shampoo. Something rich and gentle will do to be kind to your hair at the end of the day. If you're in and out of a swimming pool get some special after-swim shampoo to sort the chlorine effects out.

HOT TIP

Avoid wearing metal hair slides and clips in the hot sun. They can heat right up and give you a couple of uncomfortable hot spots. Stick to bands, scrunchies or plastic clips.

Style It
Bored with your look? Try a new one!

Long Hair
TeddyEars (you'll need four hair bands and a few grips)
1. Separate your hair into two sections with a straight parting down the middle.
2. Put each side up into a high bunch.

3. Twist one side into a rope, then twist that around on itself until your have your 'ear'.
4. Wrap the second band around the outside – this should be a nice band as it will be visible.

5. Secure any loose bit with your grips.
6. Repeat on other side.
7. Spray the whole lot with hairspray to keep it in place.

Variation - braid/plait the hair at stage 3. Use different bands with bits and bobbles on them to dress up this style. Divide your hair into three or four sections for extra knobs on!

Medium Hair
Renaissance Braids
If your hair's not really long enough to plait/braid but you would like to make a bit of a feature of it, try these.
1. Section off two wide lengths at the front of your hair.
2. Around the top of each tie a thin ribbon (the sort you use for wrapping presents works well!) It should be twice the length of the hair section and should be tied in the middle of the ribbon so that you have two equal lengths

to work with.

3. Twist the two lengths of ribbon around the hair section in opposite directions.
4. Tie off at the bottom and snip any excess.

Variation - pull the two lengths over the top of your head sideways and secure at either end with a funky clip.

Short Hair
Clip It
Unless you've got a complete crew cut, you can still have a lot of fun styling short hair.
1. Take a chunk of hair at a time, twist it and clip it.
2. Go over your whole head doing this (you might need help!)

Variation - push your hair up and back and then clip it around in a circle so that the front section is smooth and the bit on top is fluffed up and spikey!

Thread Dreads
Fancy a multi-colored cooler-than-cool thread braid in your tresses? Here's how:
Gather together lots of different, brightly colored embroidery thread. Ask Granny if she's got any off-cuts!
A pair of scissors
A piece of cardboard (3 inches/7cm square) – a bit of old cereal box'll do!

1. Cut a slit to the middle of the card.
2. Stick your scissors in the middle and wiggle them so that there's a more defined hole.
3. Cut a length of thread. It should be about three times longer than the section of hair you're going to braid.

4. Section off a strand of hair (not too thick) and brush it smooth. Then slip it through the cut in the card so that it rests snugly in the hole in the middle. Do this near the roots of the hair rather than at the end.
5. Tie the thread tightly at the top of the hair, near your cardboard shield, with a secure double knot.

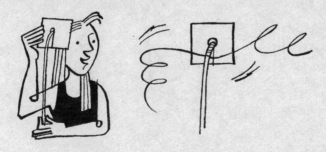

6. Start to wind the thread tightly around the hair. Hold the hair stretched out with one hand and bind with the other. If spaces appear, push the thread up to cover them.

7. Add on different colored thread whenever you fancy a change and bind round it to cover the knot.

8. Bind to the end and then tie off with a double knot.

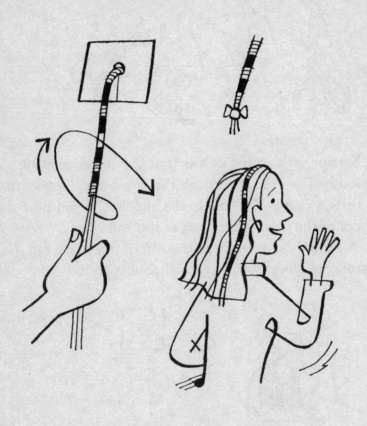

Hair Care or Scare?

Are you Queen of the Coiffure, or a stylist's worst nightmare? Find out here.

1. When you wash your hair you:
A. Use about half the bottle of shampoo, put all your hair on top of your head and rub for dear life?
B. Use a small dollop of shampoo, work mainly on the roots and let the lather run down over your hair?
C. Use soap, I can't be bothered to shampoo?

2. You think conditioner is:
A. Something for suckers?
B. Something to use once in a while – a special treat?
C. An integral part of your hair-care routine?

3. After washing your hair do you:
A. Leap straight out of the shower, pull a brush through it and then get the blow-dryer straight on it on its fastest and hottest setting?

B. Gently towel dry your hair, removing the excess moisture before slowly blow-drying it on a low heat?

C. I told you, I don't wash my hair!

4. You want to give your hair some extra body. Do you:

A. Use a bit of mousse after washing?

B. Use some wax once your hair is dry?

C. Not wash your hair for a couple of weeks?

5. Your split-end problem is getting really bad. Do you:

A. Make an appointment at the hairdressers for a chop asap?

B. Buy a year's supply of serum – that should stick the critters together?

C. Leave them as they are, you rather like the frizzy look?

6. You're feeling very dull and dreary and want a hair make-over. Do you:

A. Save up the money to go to a fancy salon and get a really good re-style?

B. Buy a couple of wash-in wash-out colorants? They should perk you up a bit!

C. Shave off all your hair? Well, it's certainly different!

7. Do you pick your hair style by:

A. Getting your mom to put a bowl on your head and cut round it? If it was good enough for medieval monks, it's certainly good enough for you!

B. Having a long hard look in the mirror and a long hard think about what would suit you, won't break the bank and need a team of on-line hairdressers to keep looking swish?

C. Observing the current trends in hairdressing techniques, trawling through magazines and checking out the top celebs' latest 'dos'?

8. Do you think Carmen Rollers are:

A. A brand of heated rollers?

B. A Bizet opera done on roller-skates?

C. A brand of Velcro rollers?

9. Your best friend's in a state of distress. She's had her lovely long hair layered and she hates it. Do you:

A. Go into overdrive with your styling sticks and clips and leave her looking better than ever?

B. Lend her a couple of scrunchies and tell her it'll grow out in no time at all?

C. Tell her to stop whining and put a hat on?

10. If you could have any hair in the world would it be:

A. Who cares, it grows out in about a week anyway?

B. A gamin crop? Simple and chic and easy to maintain.

C. Luscious, long locks? You could have them down and sleek or piled up and vampish. Oh the hours you could spend...

Your Style-wise Scores

1. A5 B10 C2 2. A2 B6 C10 3. A6 B10 C2
4. A10 B6 C2 5. A10 B6 C2
6. A10 B7 C2 7. A2B6 C10 8. A10 B2 C6
9. A10 B7 C2 10. A2 B7 C10

68-100 Coiffure Queen

Oooh you really know your crimpers from your curlers and you're not ashamed to say so. You must have really well-loved locks. But hey, don't get obsessed, OK. It's fine to care about your tresses but every now and then be prepared to just let them hang!

35-67 Hairy Fairy

You care about your hair but you're not going to let it rule your life. You know how and when to give it a lift but you're not going to make it a full-time job. Good for you!

0-34 Hair Horror

Uh-oh urgent hair-help needed. Granted, it ain't great to be a super-vain pain, but hey girl, have some pride why don't you! You are a beauty-school drop-out of the highest order. Back to the beginning of the chapter please – you've got some serious revision to do!

7. Make It Up

Make-up can be fun. Dipping into delicious little pots of different colors and textures and learning how to work with your face is great. But it's not something you need to use every day. Your beauty will be a reflection of your health and vitality and your positive attitude to life – not something you can paint on as an afterthought. But every now and again, it's fun to slap some face paint on for a special occasion – you can go from glitzy-glam for your best girlfriend's party to subtle sophistication for a fancy meal out with the family. Or go for the natural look and make the most of what's already there!

Concealers

Most bases and foundations are too heavy for young skin (they're designed to cover the creases that only come with age – yikes!). But, now and then when you only want to disguise the odd blemish, concealers are just the job.

They usually come in a stick or wand form. They are not for use as a general base or cover. They are simply there to cover up the odd blemish or blotch that you might be feeling a bit self-conscious about. They have a pretty thick consistency and are used for intensive coverage so be sure to find one that really matches your skin-tone, as one that doesn't will draw more attention to an area rather than hiding it! If you can afford it, buy a couple of concealers – one a shade lighter than your basic complexion, as different areas of your face are different colors and at times you'll be looking a bit paler than usual anyway. And if you want a really natural cover-up, try mixing a bit of concealer with a bit of foundation and applying it really lightly to the blemishes. Always use your little finger to apply, rather than going straight for the spot with the stick – you don't want to spread infection by transferring bacteria from one area to another on the stick, now do you?

Remember
- With all bases and concealers the most important thing at the end of the day is that you wash them off really thoroughly. Any traces of residual make-up will block your pores and lead to the dreaded pimple-ization of your face.
- Also, always wash your face before applying con-

cealer too — otherwise you'll just rub surface dirt deeper into your pores and then seal it in with a nice layer of make-up.

Lip Tips

Pucker up and keep your lips kissing sweet with these top tips for hot lips:

1. Grab a clean, old toothbrush (dry at the time please) and give your lips a gentle rub-down with it. This will lift off any dry and dead skin and leave your lips zingy and smooth. Remember gently does it though!
2. Slick on some yummy lip balm/gloss. You can even use good old Vaseline if you like!
3. Blot with a tissue to remove any excess grease.

Hey-presto! One set of mint-condition lips quick as you like!

If you want to apply color to your lips, it's always best to use a lip-brush. You can get a more defined outline and the lipstick will stay in place for longer. The type of lip color you use is up to you and, to a certain extent, dictated by fashion: sometimes glossy lips are where it's at, other times lips that look chalky and matt are considered in vogue. Here's the best way to have luscious lips that stay:

• Outline the bottom lip first (either with a lip-pencil or with your lip-brush). Go from the center to the right-hand corner and then from the center to the left-hand corner.

• Outline the upper lip the same way.

• Fill in with color, using your lip-brush. Make sure, if you used a lip-pencil, that the pencil and lipstick colors blend; they shouldn't appear as separate colors. Be careful to stay within the outline.

• Blot your lips on a tissue and then put a final light coat on top.

• If you want to gloss your lips apply it now over the top, but don't go right to the edge of your lips as it may make the lipstick bleed out around the edges.

HOT TIP

★ Don't try to change the shape of your lips by drawing in a lip shape you would like with the pencil and filling it in. It will appear very obvious and look a bit bizarre!

Gadget Corner

Lip-brushes

Why, why, why, you may wonder, when a lipstick is a perfectly functioning item? True, we reply, but for mixing lip color together and creating a good strong line with added staying power – you can't beat a good lip-brush. They come in a number of different sizes so try out a few and find out which is best for you. And, for real top of the range, get a retractable one – it saves having to scrabble around on the bathroom floor when you drop the lid and keeps all that sticky lippy off the inside of your make-up bag.

Glitter Girl

Glitter is gorgeous for a sparkling evening out. It can glam up anything and leave you feeling more special than a fairy princess! Here's some hot glitter know-how...

• If you've got glitter in gel form, keep it in the fridge. It'll keep it in mint condition and give it a lovely refreshing feel when you put it on.

• Don't over-do it. Your glitter will look more effective and striking if you apply it in a couple of select places, rather than smearing it all over!

• Only use glitter products that are specifically designed to be worn on the skin – anything else could cause a nasty rash.

• You can put glitter anywhere, but be sure to avoid getting any in your eyes – that smarts! Don't rub your eyes with a glittery finger, whatever you do.

• A dab of glitter on the old cheekbones will give added definition to your face.

• Pop a spot of glitter in the center of your bottom lip – and hey-presto, that's one heavenly pout.

• If you've put glitter on your bod and you don't want it to rub off – give yourself a quick once over with some hairspray – it'll seal the sparkle in. Best not to do this on your face, though.

Eye Eye

A lot of people regard their eyes as their best feature. And they're fabulous features when it comes to making-up too. From nearly natural to party eyes, you can have hours of fun trying out different effects to suit you and suit your mood.

Eye Shadow
These come in lots of different forms but the easiest to apply are usually the pressed powders. They have a nice

smooth, non-greasy texture and are easy to blend to achieve the look you want.

Most eye shadows will go on better and last longer if you have moisturized your skin before applying. You should make sure that you don't leave a gap between the lashes and the shadow – the shadow should butt up against the line of the lashes. Play around with colors, if you've bought a shade you don't like once you've got it on, don't worry, it may well work better if you blend it with another color.

Try a darker color on the outside edge and then compare it with a darker color on the side of your lid that's closer to your nose. Which works best for you?

Get Plucking

Be careful! Eyebrow plucking is there only for a finishing touch to tidy up the odd stray hair and possibly add definition to the line of your eyebrows – you shouldn't alter their basic form. Check your eyebrow's basic shape by brushing along the line of the hairs with an old, clean toothbrush. There may be one or two straggly hairs below the main line of the eyebrow. Pluck these out with a quick, firm tug. The idea is to neaten the brows while keeping them natural. Never, ever pluck eyebrow hairs from the top of the brow.

Eyebrow Brush / Comb

Well, you've gone to all that trouble to scrub, exfoliate, moisturize, gloss and the little hairy face caterpillars are crawling around in a most unruly fashion. OK, it's not quite as bad as that, but still it's a real finishing touch to give your brows a tidying brush and separate those lashes with a quick comb (and if you wear mascara, it'll get rid of any ugly clumping – yuck!) But the tip from top make-up artists is use a clean and dry old toothbrush to do that eyebrow thing and save yourself a couple of bucks – nice!

Flash Those Lashes

An easy-peasy way to make your lashes look all luscious and lovely is to use a little Vaseline (petroleum jelly) on them. It'll leave them looking dark and glossy and simply gorgeous. It's one of the best beauty products around as you can use it on your lips, too and run a little along the line of your eyebrows to give them shape and sheen.

Mascara

Tricky stuff, mascara, the first time anyone uses it they always end up in tears. Not because they look awful, but because they always poke themselves in the eye with the wand! Pick a shade that most reflects your natural lash color – you can even get transparent mascara, but Vaseline does the same job. Always put mascara on last if you're using other eye make-up i.e. eye shadow as it'll cover any of the powdery shadow that fell on to your lashes.

Hold a make-up mirror under your nose so that you're looking down the length of your nose into it. Then you can get the wand right to the bottom of your lashes and still see what you're doing. Do a couple of strokes down on the top of your lashes to cover any loose powder and then do a couple of long strokes from the bottom of your lashes to the ends on both eyes.

Finally for a really perfect finish – brush your lashes through with a lash comb.

HOT TIP

Don't pump the mascara wand in and out of the tube. This introduces air and will make your mascara clog up and dry out much sooner than it should.

Gadget Corner

Eyelash Curlers

Surgical-looking gadgets with scissor-like finger holes. You insert your eyelashes and squeeze the device shut around them – not too hard, you only want a slight curl, not your eyelashes to bend over backwards!

Always curl your lashes before applying mascara. You don't want your curlers to get all sticky and clogged up with old mascara.

Clean your curlers regularly. Wipe the rubber pads over with a damp tissue.

HOT TIP

Avoid sharing your mascara and eye-liners wherever possible. We know you love your friends enough to share anything with them, but doubt that includes germy eye infections! Nice!

HOT TIP

Keep your eye pencils in the fridge – it makes them much easier to sharpen!

Flash those Falsies

Having a fun night out? Giving your friends a brilliant girly makeover? Why not experiment with a set of false lashes – they totally change the way you look, are brilliant fun to try out and, when the night's over, you can simply take them off again.

They now come not only in black, but also in all kinds of sparkly party colors and, with a bit of practice, they're not too tricky to apply...

Set the pack out in front of you and make sure you've got a pair of tweezers to hand as they'll help make the whole procedure a bit easier.

Hold one of the lash strips up against your eye – if you think it looks too long give it a trim before you put it on!!

Take one of your falsies and hold it steady with your tweezers. Apply a thin line of the enclosed adhesive along the root-line of the false lashes.

Leave it for a couple of seconds so that the glue has time to get a bit tacky.

Carefully place it just above the line of your own lashes. Once you're sure it's in the right position, gently press it down with your finger, carefully pressing it from one end to the other.

Repeat the procedure with the other eye.

Now – flutter like a nutter!

A problem shared...

I've got red hair and my eyelashes are so pale they're almost invisible. It makes me look like my eyes are really tiny. I've tried using black mascara but they just looked really heavy and weird. Any tips?
Tilly, New York City

Yup – with red hair and pale lashes the chances are your skin is really pale too. So black lashes would look too heavy, as they wouldn't reflect your natural tones. Make-up should enhance what you've already got rather than trying to totally change it. Try using a brown or brown/black mascara instead. And for a really different look why not try a delicious green every-now-and-again, when you're feeling really adventurous!

Mad About Mehndi

Mehndi is the 3,000-year-old art form which uses henna to create delicate and intricate patterns on the skin. They are sort of like temporary tattoos and traditionally they were put on the hands and feet, but now it seems anything goes!

Originally used for decorative purposes on important occasions and celebrations across the Middle-East and the Indian subcontinent, it's now swept through the Western fashion industry with a vengeance and it's a real must-have look for just about anybody who's 'in'! Which is lucky for you, as it's now available in handy kit form all over the place.

Be warned though, although henna tattoos are temporary (they last around three weeks) as soon as the stuff touches your skin, it stains it. So, have a practice before you start and make sure you've got a clear idea of what you want and a really steady hand before you get going!

Henna can be messy and fiddly, but if you take it steady and persevere, the results can be worth it. With colors ranging from a burnt orange to a blacky-brown you can be really creative and make some really lovely designs. Try to pick a kit that includes some design sheets and then you can copy some ideas without having to struggle to come up with your own.

Where do you want it? You can happily put henna on anywhere you like. How about a bracelet design on your wrist or ankle or even around your upper arm? You can have a pattern running up your ankle bone, or go the whole hog and have a design that wraps right around your midriff! Perhaps better not to start with that. But remember, it's gonna be on for three whole weeks, not just the one night out, so if you want it strictly for partying, why not go for your shoulder-blade or collar-bone, so that it can be seen when you're wearing that little strappy number, but is hidden all week long under your school clothes!

So, want to give it a try? Here's how:
- Buy your kit (doh!). It's best to apply your henna at least 12 hours before you intend to flash your tat, so it's really a night-before job.
- Put an old towel down where you intend to be working. Although the henna is usually well contained, it does stain all it touches, so it's better safe than sorry!

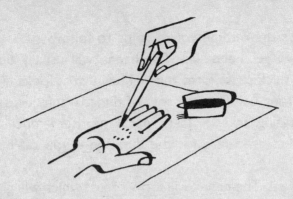

• Choose your design. Traditionally some symbols have a meaning – a lotus is for purity, a peacock for passion and a coconut for fertility – so be careful what you choose!

• Have a wash. Make sure the bit of skin you've picked to paint is clean and dry. Then rub it over with mehlabiya oil (should be included in the kit).

• Transfer. If you're using a design sheet (probably a good idea the first few times – go freehand later once you've got the hang of it) place the transfer on the skin for around 30 seconds, peel it off, and there's the outline you're going to follow.

• Now, get henna-ing. The henna will usually be in quite thick paste form and will be in what looks like a little icing bag (like the sort of thing Granny uses for decorating cakes!). Take your time. Remember any mistakes are there for the duration – you can't rub them out!

• Leave it. The henna will form a crust which will gradually flake off revealing the stained skin underneath. If you leave it alone and don't pick at it you should get the best results. The color will develop further over the next two days and then will gradually wear off as your skin slews over the following few weeks.

Temporary Tattoos

Fancy something a bit different but don't want to be stuck with it for life? Why not try a temporary tattoo, from classic designs to sophisticated patterns and cartoony funsters, you can get it all.

They're really easy to apply and if you get fed up with them usually rub off with bit of baby oil and a cotton ball.

Bindi Bonkers

Bindis are the self-adhesive decorative body jewels which Asian women have, for centuries, stuck onto their foreheads to signify their marital status – kinda like wearing a wedding ring really.

They come in all shapes, sizes and designs from a plain-colored dot to an intricately patterned diamond. And you can put them anywhere. They even look good stuck onto your fingernails.

It's cool too to put one just above the bridge of your nose and then do a line either side, following the line of your eyebrows, of much smaller glittery gems. And if they're not self-sticking, a small amount of Vaseline should do the trick.

Body Art Pencils

These come in a variety of colors (including blue, black, red and green). They look like most other make-up pencils and you can have hours of fun drawing on your own designs. They are temporary and will smudge if treated too roughly, so are best for warm evenings when you're not going to be pulling your woolly sweater on and off all night!

Nice Nails!

Here are the basics for keeping your nails in shape and slapping on that polish.

- Wash your hands and make sure your nails are clean. Use a nail brush if necessary.
- Gently file your nails in one direction only. If you go two ways, you'll weaken them and make them more likely to split. Go for a natural rounded look – even falsies aren't pointy!
- Give your nails a wipe over with a damp cotton ball, to lift off the loose bits left from filing. It'll also reveal any left-over snaggles.
- Paint 'em! Apply a clear undercoat first. This protects your nails and stops the color from your chosen polish seeping into them.
- Remember – always let each coat dry thoroughly before applying the next.
- Paint each nail in three, even strokes; one down the middle, then one down each side.

If you mess up, don't worry, just have a plentiful supply of nail-polish remover and cotton balls at the ready and you can take it off and try again!

Don't – pick your nail-polish off – it looks icky and it's bad for your nails.

Don't – use wet nail-polish to take old nail-polish off – it's too sticky and you'll get in a mess.

HOT TIP

 If your nails have been stained by deeply-colored polish, try rubbing half a lemon over them. It should make the problem a little less obvious! Or how about giving them a clean with smokers' toothpaste – nice!

Emery Boards

A must-have in every make-up bag – there's nothing worse than walking around all day with an irritatingly snaggy nail. Remember – always file in one direction only and start from the edge of the nail to the center before doing the other side. Avoid metal nail files – they're just too tough!

HOT TIP

If you've got a fave color of nail polish and it's gone all thick and sticky, try adding a couple of drops of nail-polish remover to it. Shake it up and try it out. It should thin it out a bit and revitalize that crusty old bottle.

A problem shared...

I can't stop biting my nails. I know it looks awful – when I'm doing it and the finished result – but I can't seem to stop myself. I just do it without thinking. My hands look so ugly I don't ever want to wear nail-polish or rings or anything that'll draw attention to them. How can I stop nibbling and start growing my nails?

Indira, Chicago

Why not get yourself some gross-tasting nail polish. You can get them from the pharmacy or drug store, you apply them like normal nail-polish but the moment you try to nibble you get the most gag taste in your mouth – ever. Believe me, you'll soon unlearn the old habit. If you can't quite face such drastic tactics, why don't you go for plan B. Paint up your nails nicely, put some nail transfers on them, even wear some rings. Draw attention to your hands and learn to love your nails. You won't want to spoil all your hard work by chewing on it, now will you?

HOT TIP

Get mom to move the carrots over and store your nail-polishes in the fridge. They'll last longer, go on smoother and dry quicker. Now that tip is cool!

HOT TIP

If you think your nails look a bit on the wide side, create the appearance of slimmer nails by just coloring in the middle three-quarters of each nail and leaving the outer edge bare. This works especially well with darker colored polish.

If you have big hands and you want to make them look smaller - paint your nails. It works - honest!

Paint Jobs

If your nails lack luster why not glam them up with a fresh paint job? Get together with some friends and make sure you bring at least three nail polishes each. You'll each need a fine paintbrush too (you can get one from any artists' supply shop). Give yourselves a manicure so your nails are clean and ready for action, then get painting.

• For an easy, eye-catching design, pick three colors and paint your nails in order, each nail with a different color. Dab them on a clean piece of paper first to see the combinations that work best.

• Blooming marvelous – little flowers always look lovely and they're really easy to do. First decide if you want light flowers on a dark base, or dark flowers on a light base and pick your colors accordingly. You'll need three in total. Paint your chosen base onto your nails. You'll need a couple of coats. The most important thing about nail art is that you let each layer dry thoroughly before you do the next one, so leave plenty of time. Once your base is dry start on your flowers. Dot on the flower centers first – two or three flowers is probably all that will fit on a nail – remember you've got to leave room for the petals. Once the centers have dried, put five dots, in a different color, around the outside of them, and there you have it – blooming lovely nails!
• Stripe it up. Put one shade down as a base and

then stripe another color over it from the root to the tip of your nail. Or, go the other way and stripe a color width-ways along the tip of your nails. You can even do a lightning flash zigzag diagonally across your nails if you're feeling brave enough!

• Stick it. When you've put your nail-polish on, initially it's a bit sticky — why not make use of this amazing natural phenomenon by sticking a bindi or a tiny gem onto the tip of your nails? Use a wet orange stick to pick up and position the stones.

HOT TIP

★ If you really are all thumbs and can't handle the thought of putting an eye-catching design on your nails yourself, you can now buy false nails that are already decorated to save you the bother. Phew!

8. Smells Good

The way you smell says something about you. Smells are very good at evoking memories, provoking different feelings and capturing a mood perfectly. How often has a scent carried you back to another place in your memory in a way that a picture never could? Scents are fun and you can have fun finding one that suits you. You don't have to go for the most expensive Parisian pong to smell great, there are loads of essential oils available at very reasonable prices that smell divine and can say everything about you that you might want to say.

What Scent Are You?

1. When you go to the movies do you pick:

A. A comedy – you always did like a laugh?

B. A romance – ah, there's nothing nicer than that first kiss?

C. A rugged outdoor adventure?

D. A complicated thriller set in sultry foreign climes?

2. If you could pick one of the following to chow-down on, what would it be:

A. A leafy salad, with fresh tomatoes and a light vinaigrette dressing?

B. A hot, gooey cinnamon bun?

C. A large bowl of strawberries with a dollop of whipped cream?

D. Some rich chocolate brownies?

3. If you could have the room of your dreams, what would you go for:

A. Pink and white, lovely lace trim on your bedding

and pretty print curtains?

B. Clean and chrome – no clutter, straight lines and lots of natural light?

C. Ethnic chic – lots of rich fabrics and throws and rattan and wooden furniture?

D. Bright and happy – oranges and yellows are the shades for you; bright and bold and cheery?

4. Your ideal vacation location would be:

A. India. Wonderful food, vivid colors – bright, exotic and exciting?

B. Sailing. You could really get away from it all – the wind in your hair, and nothing between you and the clear blue sky?

C. A cottage in France – warm sunlight, bees buzzing, and the fields alive with blossoming wild flowers?

D. A beach in a tropical paradise?

5. You're going to be a bridesmaid at your cousin's wedding. You get to pick your outfit. Is it:

A. Bluey-gray, shot silk, with clean straight lines – very modern and very you?

B. A fairy-princess gown – it's not every day you get to dress up like this – you're certainly going to make the most of it?

C. A cheerful, little fifties number – nipped in at the waist with a large, circle-skirt in a delicious hot pink?

D. A deep crimson long dress, with large flowing sleeves and gold-brocade detail?

Your Scent-sational Scores

3. A7 B0 C10 D4 4. A10 B7 C2 D7

1. A4 B7 C0 D10 2. A0 B10 C4 D7

0-12 Crisp 'n' Clean

You're a thoroughly modern miss. You like fresh air and wide open spaces. You favor cool colors like white and silver and need a scent to reflect your outlook on life. Go for oceanic clean crisp perfumes which will sum up the real you in one sniff.

13-25 Fruity

You're a happy-go-lucky kind of a gal. You like delicious scents of summer fruits and the feel of warm sunshine on your skin. Go for happy, fruity scents that will suit your personality down to the ground.

26-38 Floral

Ahh - what a romantic. Your idea of heaven would

be to skip through a summer meadow alive with the scent of wild flowers. You like delicate pastels and floaty fabrics and need a scent to complement your look. Go for floral tones, they'll speak volumes for you.

39-50 Spicy

You're a vibrant adventurous soul. You love rich colors, spicy foods and strong, musky scents. Warm, exotic perfumes will be just right for you.

How to Test a Perfume

• Don't test more than two scents at any one time – your nose will numb out with any more!

• Sniff the bottle before you spritz. You'll get the scent's 'top note' which will give an idea of what it's going to smell like. If you like that, you may well like the perfume.

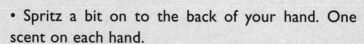

• Spritz a bit on to the back of your hand. One scent on each hand.

• Don't rub it, let the alcohol evaporate off and the scent will cling to your skin.

• Don't smell it straight away, it will be far too strong and overpowering. Walk around with it for at least half an hour and then give it a sniff. It will have had time to settle into the scent it's going to be on you.

• Wait another half an hour and sniff again. Scents often become sweeter over time – you may not like the finished result. But, if you do, this may be the scent for you!

HOT TIP

No perfume smells exactly the same on any two people so don't buy a perfume just because it smells fantastic on your best friend. Check it out yourself first and if it suits you too – go for it!

HOT TIP

Too poor to buy expensive perfumes? Fear not, if you know you've got a big night ahead of you get down to your local department store and spritz yourself with your favorite designer scent. By the time the party comes around it will have settled into the divine and delicate aroma you want it to be ...and all for free!

Stink Alert!

Remember – you will become used to the smell of your perfume and may even not notice it any more. It's still there though and you still smell delicious so, don't put any more on, it'll be stronger than you think and people'll think you stink!

HOT TIP

Avoid wearing perfume if you're going to lie out in the sun, some can contain ingredients that might not react well in sunlight and you could end up with an irritated patch or a nasty rash.

HOT TIP

Don't squirt your perfume directly onto your clothes, it could stain them. And definitely don't use perfume to try to cover up the smell of sweat – the two things will simply react together and the end result will be far from the pleasant aroma you had hoped for!

DIY Treats

How about making your own perfumes for some simply lovely natural aromas? You hardly need any ingredients at all and some of them you can even nab from the garden. Remember when you're done to store your scent out of direct sunlight. If you keep your bottles in a cool, dark place it'll help to keep your scent lovely and fresh.

Lavender Toilet Water
I tablespoon oil of lavender
4 cups ethyl alcohol
(available from pharmacies)
I dessertspoon rose water

Mix the lavender oil with a little alcohol until blended, then slowly add the remainder. Lastly stir in the rose water. Put it into a sealed bottle/container and leave for six weeks to reach maturity.

Cologne Water

2 teaspoons lavender oil
3 teaspoons clove oil
2 cups ethyl alcohol
2 tablespoons rose water

Blend the two oils with a little of the alcohol until everything is well mixed together. Mix in the last of the alcohol and add the rose water. Bottle and store for six to eight weeks until mature.

Rose Essence

3 handfuls of dried rose petals
3 tablespoons sweet almond oil

Put the dried rose petals in a glass (heatproof) bowl and cover with the oil. Place the bowl in a pan of simmering water and heat until the oil has removed all the color from the petals. Strain. Keep in a container with a well-sealed lid.

Layering

If you want your chosen scent to last for as long as poss, try layering. If you can get soap, shower gel and body lotion all with the same fragrance, you build up layers of the scent which will mean it will go on for longer. Also, by trying to use products with the same aroma, you'll avoid any unpleasant clashes!

9. Best Feet Forward!

It's pedicure time!

Give your feet a real treat. You run around on them, stand on them, dance about on them and then ... ignore them completely. Looking after your feet can actually be good fun and very, very soothing. Look after your feet and you'll have a new spring in your step before you know it!

Take the time when you're having a nice soak in the tub to give your feet a treat. Have your pumice stone at the ready and when the hard skin has softened up a bit give it a gentle rub to lift away those nasty dead skin cells that build up on your poor old tootsies. You can also buy exfoliating scrubs especially for your feet.

Once you've dried up, why not give your feet a soothing massage with some invigorating foot balm. Aniseed, menthol and minty aromas are just perfect to leave your feet feeling refreshed and invigorated.

Here's how to give yourself a lovely foot massage. And if you're not in the mood, you can always get someone else to give you a soothing treat instead ...You can do this dry or with a little bit of massage oil, or soothing foot lotion.

- Sit in a comfortable cross-legged position with one of your feet sole upwards in your lap.

- Hold your foot in both hands for thirty seconds.

- Relax your foot with a light wobbling motion.

- Run your thumbs, one after the other, up the length of the foot.

- Squeeze gently, with small circular motions on the ball of your foot.

- Apply pressure with your thumb and run it along the arch of your foot.

- Rotate, twist and pull each toe gently.

- Squeeze gently the flesh in between each of your toes.

• Sandwich your foot between your hands and slide them off gently.

• Quietly hold your foot for thirty seconds.

• Repeat on other foot.

Gadget Corner

Toe Separators

Cheap and cheerful, these spongy little fellas are there to help you with the tricky business of painting your toenails. There's nothing more disappointing than going for the glamour of painted toenails and ending up looking like you've dipped your tootsies in a tub of paint. Keep the little piggies apart and you'll find polish a breeze. You can of course use sausage shapes of cotton balls to do the same thing – what a great money-saving idea, guys!

Pumice Stone

Now, we're talking hard dry skin here. No, not on your face – on your feet. But, never fear, pumice is here. There's nothing nicer than soaking in the tub and giving your feet a refreshing rub down with a bit of the rough stuff. It'll ease off dry and dead skin and leave your tootsies feeling fresh and full of spring.

Toenail Clippers

Toenail clippers, unlike scissors, cut the nails across in a perfectly straight line. They are also good and strong to deal with toughy big-toe nails. Toenails need to be cut in this way as it prevents the nail cutting into the flesh and also stops ingrowing toenails.

Common Footy Problems

Athlete's Foot

This is a fungal infection. You can pick it up (like verrucas/warts) by walking around in the dressing rooms in your bare feet. It's called athlete's foot because it loves warm, damp environments and commonly appears between the toes or on the soles of the feet. You'll know you've got it if you have itchy, flaky skin on your feet. It's hard to prevent getting it, but it's pretty easy to treat. Your pharmacist will be able to give you some over-the-counter remedies and if that doesn't work the doctor or chiropodist will know just what to do.

Verrucas/Warts

Verrucas/warts are actually caused by a virus, which manages to wiggle its wily way into your epidermal skin cells. Verrucas/warts can be very painful and are highly contagious so definitely DON'T go swimming when you've got one.

Verrucas/warts can be very easily treated with over-the-counter medications. Usually they work by eroding the dead skin cells and in so doing taking the nasty verruca with them. If you really can't get rid of your verruca on your own – see the doc, she'll be able to sort you out with a more permanent cure.

Corns

These are localized areas of hard skin that's built up over time, usually because of friction and rubbing. Here's one great reason for wearing well-fitting comfortable shoes. It's easy to avoid getting corns by looking after your feet from day one. But if you do get them, get them looked at by a professional chiropodist pronto, and DON'T attempt to do any corn-removing surgery yourself.

Calluses

These are like corns in that they are caused by friction or pressure. So, again, avoid getting them in the first place by being choosy about what you put on your feet. But, if it's already too late for that, start now with your foot care. After you've had a lovely bath, get to work with that pumice stone on your softened skin and gently work those calluses away.

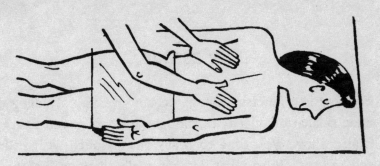

10. The Inner You!

Let's face it, feeling great isn't just about feeling *physically* great, is it? Nope, it's about an emotional state too. Your body might be in tip-top condition but if you're stressed and depressed you're not *really* feeling great are you?!

A lot of the things that have been touched on in previous chapters will have an effect on your mental state: exercise gives you a natural happy buzz; making yourself look nice makes you feel special and confident; wearing a particular perfume can accentuate your mood; having a facial sauna or a foot massage helps you to relax and feel soothed after a long day. But, there are lots of things designed especially to deal with stress and help you really focus on the inner you – working on feeling really wonderful from the inside out!

Massage

Massage is a fantastic thing! It can give you a feeling of deep relaxation, clarity of thought and a renewed energy. It also allows you time to really get in touch with yourself and tune in to what you are really thinking. The best thing is, depending on the area you want to massage, you can do it on yourself! But if you want a back massage you may need to enlist the help of a friend – choose someone you feel relaxed and comfortable with and remember, if your best buddy's taken the time and effort to give you a lovely massage, it's only polite that you give her one back!

Remember - you can massage through clothing if you like, but it works better skin on skin. If you're not keen on getting all oily you can massage dry (with no oil) but again, it's more successful with. You don't need any expensive massage oil, any vegetable oil will do! Don't use baby oil – it's not grainy enough and is therefore too slippery!

Self Massage
Face
• Hold your hands to the side of your face for a quiet moment.

• Put your thumbs in the middle of your forehead and drag them slowly outwards towards your temples – repeat x 5.

• Starting from the top of your nose use the middle finger of each hand to apply a little pressure, then move along and outwards applying a little pressure each time you move your fingers. Once you get to your temples, move back into the middle, but higher up and repeat until you've covered your whole forehead.

• Stroke from the middle of your nose over your eyebrows and when you reach your temples, circle gently on your temples.

• Stroke gently down your nose x 5.

• Circle around your cheeks – this is nice and squidgy!

• Using both hands, overlapping one after the other, knead your chin with a stroking motion.

• With small, gentle grabbing motions work along your lower jawbone. Your jaw has a habit of becoming clenched with tension – this is a good way to relax it.

• Make a final connection – holding your hands lightly to the side of your face for another quiet moment.

• Throughout – Don't forget to breathe!!

(for foot massage see p 141)

Massage With a Friend

Giving a Massage
- Make sure the receiver is comfortable and warm.
- Make sure they'll tell you if your touch is too light or too hard.
- Make sure you adjust your touch if they say it's too light or too hard!
- Remember giving can be just as nice as receiving!

Receiving a Massage
- Relax!
- If something is not comfortable – tell your giver.
- Be aware of your breathing and focus on the parts of you that move as you breathe in and out.
- Let go of any worries on your mind and focus on the feeling of the massage.

Back

The receiver should lie on their stomach with their arms down by their side and their head to one side. The giver should make sure the receiver is comfortable before starting. The giver should kneel, or squat, or sit however is comfortable for them at the receiver's head.

• Firstly, place your hands gently but firmly at the top of your friend's back. Hold them quietly there for a moment to establish contact.

• Glide your hands slowly from the top of the back down to the bottom then back up the sides to the top again. Repeat x 5.

• Don't forget to check with your friend that the amount of pressure you're using is OK. You don't want to squeeze the living daylights out of her!

• Make broad circling motions down from the top of the back to the bottom and then back up again from the bottom to the top.

• Using your thumbs only, one after the other, in small strokes, make an overlapping pattern across the top of the shoulders. Continue over the rest of the back.

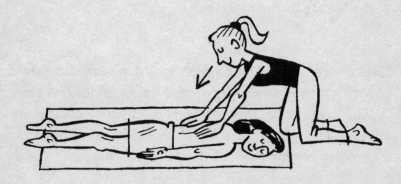

- Make small circles from the bottom of the back up the whole spine.
- Repeat the first gliding motion x 5.

- Stroke down from the shoulders down the fore-arms and whisk off.
- Place your hands quietly on the top of your friend's back for a couple of moments for a final connection.

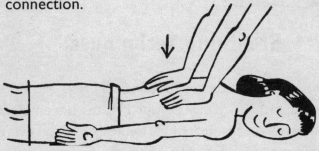

Mmmmm, doesn't that feel better?!

Aromatherapy

This can be used in conjunction with massage or on its own. As the word suggests aroma-therapy is to do with smells! Different smells can affect us in different ways – from deeply relaxing to very stimulating. You can buy essential oils and concentrated essences from lots of health food shops and alternative gift stores. Read carefully what the different scents can do for you and enjoy! Remember though, essential oil is pretty heady stuff, so you'll only need to use a tiny bit at a time!

Breathing Techniques

When you feel upset or in a bit of a panic, you may notice that your breathing changes. Your breaths become shallower and faster, your heart beats quickly – if you can get a grip on your breathing, you'll begin to feel a lot calmer almost instantly. Here are some great relaxation techniques to help you feel better in times of stress or just in general!

Quick Relaxation Technique

When you need to calm yourself down – just before you take a test or have to speak in public – try out this quick breathing technique to help you feel calm, collected and in control.

- Find a quiet space.
- Breathe in and out three times. Take a count of four for each inward and outward breath.
- On the first inward breath think 'peace'.
- On the first outward breath think 'quiet'.
- On the second inward breath think 'peace'.
- On the second outward breath think 'calm'.
- On the third inward breath think 'peace'.
- On the third outward breath think 'tranquility'.

On each outward breath be aware of your shoulders, try to let them sink naturally down rather than being tensed up around your ears. How much calmer do you feel? Loads, I bet!

Deep Relaxation Technique

It's best to do this when you go to bed at night as it can lead to sleep! But you can take time out in the day if you'd like some real 'me' time! You will need to set aside a bit of quiet time though, when you know no one's going to start hollering for you halfway through!

• Lie on your back with your arms and legs out straight — but not tensed. Take two slow, deep breaths in and out and be aware of your body's contact with the surface you're lying on and try to empty your mind of any thoughts left over from the day.

• Continue to breathe deeply throughout.

• Go through every part of your body from your head to your toes tensing each part and then relaxing it completely as follows:

> • Head (scrunch up face, raise eyebrows and relax).
>
> • Shoulders (raise up to your ears then let flop back down).
>
> • Torso (squeeze arms in and tense tummy muscles then release).
>
> • Arms (tense arms and clench fists then release).
>
> • Butt (clench and relax).
>
> • Legs (turn feet up and tense legs then release).
>
> • Feet (point toes hard then release).
>
> • You should be feeling more relaxed already.

• Breathe in and out slowly. Concentrate on the parts of your body that move when you breathe and try to empty your mind of any lingering worries.

• Imagine a place you would love to be, somewhere warm and comfortable and safe where you feel completely relaxed. Breathe the air of that place.

• Feel the warmth of that place.

• Continue to breathe slowly in and out until you drift into sleep.

If you are doing this in the day acknowledge when you want to stop then give yourself a minute or two breathing slowly before you sit up. Sit up slowly and take a little time to stretch and come back round to the day.

It's important to find some time in your life to do some proper relaxing. Sorry, but watching TV doesn't really count – it's actually a stimulant and doesn't provide you with any space to think or just be quiet for a while. So have a go at some real relaxation.

All of these techniques promote positive feelings within you that promote good health and well-being and that can't be bad!

So Just How Body Wise Are You?

You've read it all and maybe even done some of it too. But has it been absorbed like a good moisturizer or did it flake right off you like so much dead skin? Take the test and see...

1. Moisturizer:

A. Puts moisture back into your skin?

B. Helps seal in the skin's natural moisture?

C. Is only for old people?

2. Dandruff is:

A. A sign of a dirty head?

B. One of the most common skin complaints around?

C. Really, really difficult to get rid of?

3. A pumice stone is:

A. Something you use to rub dead skin off your feet?

B. Something you use to file your nails?

C. Something you use to massage your feet?

4. Exfoliating is:

A. Good for your skin – you should do it every day?

B. Bad for your skin – you shouldn't ever do it?

C. Good for your skin – but once a week's enough?

5. If you shave your legs the hair will:

A. Never come back?

B. Grow back the same?

C. Grow back thicker?

6. Do you exercise:

A. At least four times a week?

B. Less than four times a week?

C. Never?

7. Do you eat at least one piece of fresh fruit:

A. Never?

B. At least once a week but not every day?

C. Every day?

8. What is a bindi?

A. A small sticky decoration you can stick on your face or nails.

B. A form of temporary tattoo.

C. A type of food.

9. Can you use perfume to disguise the smell of sweat?

A. If you're desperate – but it won't smell very nice.

B. No, it'll react and smell awful.

C. Yes, I do it all the time.

10. Why shouldn't you share your mascara with your buddies?

A. Because they never lend me theirs!

B. Because they might damage it.

C. Because it can transfer germs and lead to eye infections.

Your Body Wise Scores

1. A5 B10 C0   2. A0 B10 C5
3. A10 B0 C5   4. A5 B0 C10
5. A0 B10 C5   6. A10 B5 C0
7. A0 B5 C0   8. A10 B5 C0
9. A5 B10 C0   10. A0 B5 C10

0-35 Back to the Beginning

Er, hello! Did any of this stuff go in? I don't think so. You just don't know what's good for you, do ya? If you don't want to end up in serious beauty therapy – and I mean therapy – best you get yourself back to the beginning of the book and start all over again ... Chapter One awaits!

36-66 Revision Required

Mmmm not bad – you can obviously tell one end of a pair of tweezers from the other, but you're not quite as clued up as you could be. Maybe you could do with a bit of dipping just to refresh your memory here and there. You'll soon be right up there with the beauty school graduates!

67-100 You Made The Grade!

Wow – you certainly know your stuff, and what's more you put it into practise, too! Your body must be real grateful! Carry on treating it as nicely as you do and you've got a friend for life there. Nice to know you're looking good and feeling great - keep it up, you're a real body-smart star!